Active LISTENING
Second Edition

1

STEVEN BROWN
DOROLYN SMITH

CAMBRIDGE
UNIVERSITY PRESS

University Printing House, Cambridge CB2 8BS, United Kingdom

One Liberty Plaza, 20th Floor, New York, NY 10006, USA

477 Williamstown Road, Port Melbourne, VIC 3207, Australia

4843/24, 2nd Floor, Ansari Road, Daryaganj, Delhi – 110002, India

79 Anson Road, #06–04/06, Singapore 079906

Cambridge University Press is part of the University of Cambridge.

It furthers the University's mission by disseminating knowledge in the pursuit of education, learning and research at the highest international levels of excellence.

www.cambridge.org
Information on this title: www.cambridge.org/9780521678131

First published 2007
20 19 18 17 16 15

Printed in Great Britain by CPI Group (UK) Ltd, Croydon CRO 4YY

A catalogue record for this publication is available from the British Library

ISBN 978-0-521-67813-1 student's book and self-study audio CD
ISBN 978-0-521-67814-8 teacher's manual and audio CD
ISBN 978-0-521-67815-5 CDs (audio)

Art direction, book design, photo research, and layout services: Adventure House, NYC
Audio production: Full House, NYC

Contents

Plan of the book

Acknowledgments

Illustration credits

Kenneth Batelman: 50, 51
CB Canga: 72, 73, 74, 77
James Elston: 6, 31, 46, 70, 71, 78
Chuck Gonzales: 5, 38, 61
Ben Kirchner: 12

Monica Lind: 28, 29
Barbara MacGregor: 8
Frank Montagna: 21, 24, 32, 33, 54, 69
Terry Wong: 34, 43
Filip Yip: 4, 19, 52, 56

Photography credits

3 © Getty Images
7 © Punchstock
10 (*top row, both*) © Punchstock; (*middle row, left to right*) © Punchstock; © Corbis; © Alamy; © Masterfile; © Alamy; (*bottom row, all*) © Punchstock
11 (*all except bottom left*) © Punchstock; (*bottom left*) © Jack Hollingsworth/Corbis
15 (*clockwise from top left*) © Punchstock; © José Fuste Raga/zefa/Corbis; © Glen Allison/ Getty Images; © Walter Bibikow/Index Stock; © Getty Images; © Getty Images
18 © George Kerrigan
20 (*clockwise from top left*) © Alamy; © Punchstock; © Bill Bettencourt/Jupiter Images; © Punchstock; © Istock; © Punchstock; © Kyle Rothenborg/ Jupiter Images
22 © Steve Allen Travel Photography/Alamy
23 (*garlic*) © Istock; (*chicken*) © Alamy; (*tomatoes*) © Alamy; (*lemons*) © Photos.com; (*basil leaves*) © Punchstock; (*hot peppers*) © Istock; (*broccoli*) © Istock; (*bean sprouts*) © Punchstock; (*peanuts*) © Photospin; (*green onions*) © Istock; (*shrimp*) © Photos.com; (*mushrooms*) © Photospin
25 © Ron Chapple/Getty Images
26 © Getty Images
30 © Timothy O'Rourke
36 © Verna Bice/Acclaim Images
40 (*clockwise from top left*) © Jiri Rezac/Alamy; © Craig Aurness/Corbis; © Joe Raedle/ Newscom; © Lee Jin-man/AP Wide World
41 (*left to right*) © Punchstock; © Yasser Al-Zayyat/ Newscom

42 (*clockwise from top left*) © Berry Wetcher/ Columbia Tri Star/The Kobal Collection; © Bettmann/Corbis; © Touchstone/Everett Collection; © Universal/The Kobal Collection; © Sebastian D'Souza/Newscom; © Everett Collection
44 (*left to right*) © Punchstock; © Corbis
47 © Getty Images
48 (*clockwise from top left*) © Getty Images; © Punchstock; © Age fotostock; © Masterfile
58 (*clockwise from top left*) © CuboImages/Alamy; © Punchstock; © Alamy; © Alamy; © Juliet Coombe/Lonely Planet Images
59 (*left to right*) © Alamy; © Index Stock
60 (*clockwise from top left*) © Punchstock; © Punchstock; © Punchstock; © Punchstock; © Getty Images; © Reza Estakhrian/Getty Images; © Punchstock; © Juan Silva/Getty Images
62 (*clockwise from top left*) © Jeff Greenberg/Photo Edit; © Age fotostock; © Punchstock; © Jupiter Images
64 (*clockwise from top left*) © Newscom; © Joe Carini/Pacific Stock; © Collin Reid/AP Wide World; © Henry Romero/Corbis; © Bobby Yip/ Corbis; © Imagebank Sweden/Newscom
66 (*clockwise from top left*) © Kevin R. Morris/ Corbis; © Alamy; © Choi Jae-Ku/AFP/Newscom; © Peter Bowater/Alamy
68 (*puppets*) © Kathryn Burrington/Alamy
76 © Dallas Stribley/Lonely Planet Images
77 © Money Sharpa/EPA/Sipa

Author acknowledgments

We would like to thank our **reviewers** for their helpful suggestions:
Andrew Newton, **Sogang University**, Seoul, South Korea
Yao-feng Huang, **Tajen University**, Pingtung, Taiwan
Gordon Sites, **Keihoku Junior High School**, Chiba, Japan
Brooks Slaybaugh, **Tamagawa Gakuen**, Tokyo, Japan
David Philip, **Pusan National University**, Pusan, South Korea
Robert Bendergrass, **Pukyong National University**, Pusan, South Korea

We would also like to acknowledge the **students** and **teachers** in the following schools and institutes who piloted components of the first edition of *Active Listening*:

Alianza Cultural Uruguay-Estados Unidos, Montevideo, Uruguay; **Bae Centre**, Buenos Aires, Argentina; **Bunka Institute of Foreign Languages**, Tokyo, Japan; **Educational Options**, Santa Clara, California, U.S.A.; **Impact English**, Santiago, Chile; **Instituto Cultural de Idiomas Ltda.**, Caxias do Sul, Brazil; **Kansai University of Foreign Studies**, Osaka, Japan; **Koyo Choji Co. Ltd.**, Hitachi, Japan; **National Chin-Yi Institute of Technology**, Taichung, Taiwan; **Osaka Institute of Technology**, Osaka, Japan; **Southern Illinois University**, Niigata, Japan; **Suzugamine Women's College**, Hiroshima City, Japan; **Tokyo Foreign Language College**, Tokyo, Japan; **Umeda Business College**, Osaka, Japan; **University of Michigan English Language Institute**, Ann Arbor, Michigan, U.S.A.

Thanks also go to those **interviewed** for the **Expansion** units: Ayman Da'na, Larissa D'Angelo, Patsorn Janprasert, Smita Kulkarni, and Elisa Sileoni, and to the English Language Institute at the University of Pittsburgh for support during this project.

A special thanks to the **editorial** and **production** team at Cambridge University Press who worked on this edition:
Eleanor Barnes, David Bohlke, Karen Brock, Rob Freire, Deborah Goldblatt, Yuri Hara, Louisa Hellegers, Lise Minovitz, Sandra Pike, Danielle Power, Tami Savir, Jaimie Scanlon, Kayo Taguchi, Louisa van Houten, and Dorothy Zemach. This book is much better because of their careful work and helpful insights.

Thanks to the Cambridge University Press **staff** and **advisors**:
Harry Ahn, Yumiko Akeba, Michelle Kim, Andy Martin, Nigel McQuitty, Carine Mitchell, Mark O'Neil, Rebecca Ou, Bruno Paul, Dan Schulte, Catherine Shih, Howard Siegelman, and Ivan Sorrentino.

Very special thanks to Deborah Goldblatt, who has been enthusiastic about this project for longer than she would have preferred. Thanks for her patience and her support over the years.

Finally, we would like to acknowledge and thank Marc Helgesen for his role as author on the first edition. He's remained a great friend and source of ideas throughout the writing of this book.

To the teacher

Active Listening, Second Edition is a fully updated and revised edition of the popular three-level listening series for adult and young adult learners of North American English. Each level offers students 16 engaging, task-based units, each built around a topic, function, or grammatical theme. Grounded in the theory that learners are more successful listeners when they activate their prior knowledge of a topic, the series gives students a frame of reference to make predictions about what they will hear. Through a careful balance of activities, students learn to listen for main ideas, to listen for details, and to listen and make inferences.

Active Listening, Second Edition Level 1 is intended for high-beginning to low-intermediate students. It can be used as a main text for listening classes or as a component in speaking or integrated-skills classes.

The second edition differs from the first in a number of ways. In recent years, there has been a greater emphasis on the role of vocabulary and pronunciation in the field of second language acquisition. To reflect this emphasis, the second edition provides a more refined vocabulary syllabus and a more extensive preview of words. The final section of each unit has also been expanded to provide a full-page speaking activity, including pronunciation practice. In addition, the Listening tasks in each unit have been expanded. Students listen to the same input twice, each time listening for a different purpose and focusing on a listening skill appropriate for that purpose. Other changes in the second edition include the systematic integration of cultural information. Most units contain interesting cultural information in the listening tasks, and a new, two-page Expansion unit, containing cultural information about a country or region of the world and an authentic student interview, has been added after every four units to review and extend the language and topics of the previous units. Each unit also has a Self-study page, accompanied by an audio CD, that can be used for self-study or homework.

ABOUT THE BOOK

The book includes 16 core units and four expansion units. Each core unit has four parts: **Warming up**, two main **Listening tasks**, and **Your turn to talk**, a speaking activity for pairs or small groups. The four **Expansion** units present cultural information related to the unit themes. In addition, there is an introductory lesson called **Before you begin**. This lesson introduces students to helpful learning strategies and types of listening.

The units can be taught in the order presented or out of sequence to follow the themes of the class or another book it is supplementing. In general, the tasks in the second half of the book are more challenging than those in the first, and language from earlier units is recycled as the book progresses.

Unit organization

Each unit begins with an activity called **Warming up**. This activity, usually done in pairs, serves two purposes: It reminds students of what they already know about the topic, and it previews common vocabulary used in the unit. When they do the warming up activity, students use their prior knowledge, or "schema," about the topic, vocabulary, and structures, as well as learn new vocabulary and phrases that are connected to the theme of the unit. The combination of the two approaches makes the listening tasks that follow easier.

Listening task 1 and **Listening task 2** are the major listening exercises. Each task has two parts. The students work with the same input in both parts of the task, but they listen for different reasons each time. The tasks are balanced to include a variety of listening skills, which are identified in a box to the left of each listening exercise. Because *Active Listening* features a task-based approach, students should do the activities as they listen, rather than wait until they have finished listening to a particular segment. To make this easier, writing is kept to a minimum. In most cases, students check boxes, number items, circle answers, or write only words or short phrases.

Your turn to talk, the final section of each unit, is a short, fluency-oriented speaking task done in pairs or small groups. First, students *prepare* for the speaking activity by gathering ideas and thinking about the topic. Next, they *practice* a pronunciation point. Finally, they *speak* to their classmates as they exchange information or opinions.

The two-page **Expansion** unit after every four units features listening activities that provide general cultural information about a country or region of the world and an authentic interview with a person from that place. The tasks focus on the same listening skills as the core units and recycle the themes and topics of the preceding four units.

The **Self-study** page reviews language, vocabulary, and themes from the unit and provides personalization exercises. It can be used for homework or for additional listening practice in class.

Hints and techniques

■ Be sure to do the **Warming up** section for each unit. This preview can help students develop useful learning strategies. It also helps students to be more successful listeners, which, in turn, motivates and encourages them.

■ Try to play a particular segment only one or two times. If students are still having difficulty, try telling them the answers. Then play the audio again and let them experience understanding what they heard previously.

■ If some students find listening very difficult, have them do the task in pairs, helping each other as necessary. The **Teacher's Manual**, described in the box in the next column, contains additional ideas.

■ Some students may not be used to active learning. Those students may be confused by your instructions since they are used to a more passive role. Explaining activities verbally is usually the least effective way to give instructions. It is better to demonstrate. For example, read the instructions as briefly as possible (e.g., "Listen. Number the

pictures."). Then play the first part of the audio program. Stop the recording and elicit the correct answer from the students. Those who weren't sure what to do will quickly understand. The same techniques work for **Warming up** and **Your turn to talk**. Lead one pair or group through the first step of the task. As the other students watch, they will quickly see what they are supposed to do.

> *Active Listening, Second Edition* Level 1 is accompanied by a Teacher's Manual that contains step-by-step teaching notes with key words highlighted, optional speaking activities and listening strategies, photocopiable unit quizzes for each Student's Book unit, and two complete photocopiable tests with audio CD.

HOW STUDENTS LEARN TO LISTEN

Many students find listening to be one of the most difficult skills in English. The following explains some of the ideas incorporated into the book to make students become more effective listeners. *Active Listening, Second Edition* Level 1 is designed to help students make real and rapid progress. Recent research into teaching listening and its related receptive skill, reading, has given insights into how successful students learn foreign or second languages.

Bottom-up vs. top-down processing: a brick-wall analogy

To understand what our students are going through as they learn to listen or read, consider the "bottom-up vs. top-down processing" distinction. The distinction is based on the ways students process and attempt to understand what they read or hear. With bottom-up processing, students start with the component parts: words, grammar, and the like. Top-down processing is the opposite. Students start from their background knowledge.

This might be better understood by means of a metaphor. Imagine a brick wall. If you are standing at the bottom looking at the wall brick by brick, you can easily see the details. It is difficult, however, to get an overall view of the wall. And, if you come to a missing brick (e.g., an unknown word or unfamiliar structure), you're stuck. If, on the other hand, you're sitting on the top of the wall, you can easily see the landscape. Of course, because of distance, you'll miss some details.

Students, particularly those with years of "classroom English" but little experience in really using the language, try to listen from the "bottom up."

They attempt to piece the meaning together, word by word. It is difficult for us, as native and advanced non-native English users, to experience what students go through. However, try reading the following *from right to left*.

> word one ,slowly English process you When to easy is it ,now doing are you as ,time a at .word individual each of meaning the catch understand to difficult very is it ,However .passage the of meaning overall the

You were probably able to understand the paragraph:

> When you process English slowly, one word at a time, as you are doing now, it is easy to catch the meaning of each individual word. However, it is very difficult to understand the overall meaning of the passage.

While reading, however, it is likely you felt the frustration of bottom-up processing; you had to get each individual part before you could make sense of it. This is similar to what our students experience – and they're having to wrestle the meaning in a foreign language. Of course, this is an ineffective way to listen since it takes too long. While students are still trying to make sense of what has been said, the speaker keeps going. The students get lost.

Although their processing strategy makes listening difficult, students do come to class with certain strengths. From their years of English study, most have a relatively large, if passive, vocabulary. They also often have a solid receptive knowledge of English grammar. We shouldn't neglect the years of life experience; our students bring with them a wealth of background knowledge on many topics. These three strengths – vocabulary, grammar, and life experience – can be the tools for effective listening.

The **Warming up** activities in *Active Listening* build on those strengths. By engaging the students in active, meaningful prelistening tasks, students integrate bottom-up and top-down processing. They start from meaning, but, in the process of doing the task, use vocabulary and structures (grammar) connected with the task, topic, or function. The result is an integrated listening strategy.

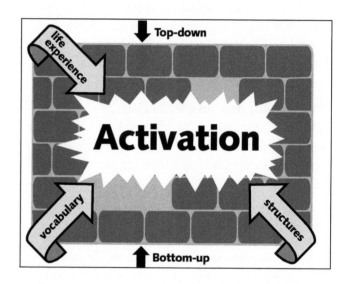

Types of listening

A second factor that is essential in creating effective listeners is exposing them to a variety of types of listening. Many students have only had experience with listening for literal comprehension. While listening for details, or specific information, is an important skill, it represents only one type. We have attempted to reach a balance in the book in order to give students experience with – and an understanding of – listening for the main idea, or gist, and listening and making inferences. Students usually are quick to understand the idea of listening for the main idea. They can easily imagine having to catch the general meaning of something they hear. Inference – listening "between the lines" – can be more difficult.

Take the following examples (from the introductory unit, **Before you begin**). The students hear the following conversation:

Paul: Hello?

Kate: Hi, Paul. This is Kate.

Paul: Oh, hi. How are you feeling? Are you still sick?

Kate: No, I feel better, thanks. I'm going to school tomorrow. What's the homework for English class?

Paul: The homework? Just a minute. . . . OK, here it is. Read pages twenty-three and twenty-four.

Kate: Twenty-three and twenty-four? OK. Thanks. See you tomorrow.

Paul: Yeah, see you tomorrow. Bye.

Students listening for the main idea, or gist, can easily identify "school" as the main topic of conversation, even though Kate and Paul also discuss the fact that Kate has been feeling sick. They are also able to pick out the specific information, or details; in this case, the page numbers for homework. To help students understand the idea of inference – listening "between the lines" – ask them whether or not both students went to school today. Even though neither speaker directly says that Kate was absent, students can understand that Kate was sick and did not go to class. Students come to understand that what they are listening for is just as important as what they are listening to.

Many of these ideas are helpful in understanding the listening process, but they should not be seen as rigid models. We need to remember that listening is actually very complex. A student listening for gist or inference may, for example, get the clues from catching a couple of specific bits of information.

Remember that although listeners need practice in listening, they also need more: They need to learn *how* to listen. They need different types of listening strategies and tasks. They need to learn to preview. Our students need exposure to it all. When students get the exposure they need, they build their listening skills. They become active listeners.

Steven Brown
Dorolyn Smith

Before you begin

Learn how to listen.

From the people who wrote this book

Dear Students:

We hope that you learn a lot of English. We also hope that you enjoy learning it.

There are many different ways to learn. This book will help you learn to listen. Think about how you learn best. Find ways that work for you.

You need to be an active listener. When you listen, do these things:

1. *Think about what you are listening to.*
   - *What is the topic?*
   - *What do you already know about the topic?*
2. *Think about what you are listening for.*
   - *What do you need to know?*
   - *What do you need to do?*
3. *When you don't understand, ask.*
   - *For example, you could say, "Could you repeat that?"*

Good luck with learning English. You can do it!

Sincerely,
Steven Brown
Dorolyn Smith

Could you repeat that?

 CLASSROOM LANGUAGE **A** Work with a partner. Complete the sentences.

What do you say when . . . ?

1 you want someone to say something again

C_ould_ you r_epeat_ that?

2 you want to hear the recording again

Once m_____ , p_____ .

3 you don't know how to spell a word

H____ d__ _____ spell (that)?

4 you want to know a word in English

H____ d__ _____ say (that) in English?

LISTEN **B** Now listen. Were you correct? Write the sentences.

1. _Could you repeat that?_

2. _____

3. _____

4. _____

Types of listening

There are many ways to listen. We listen differently for different reasons.

MAIN IDEA **A** 🎧 **Listen to the conversation. What is the most important idea?**
Check (✓) the correct answer.

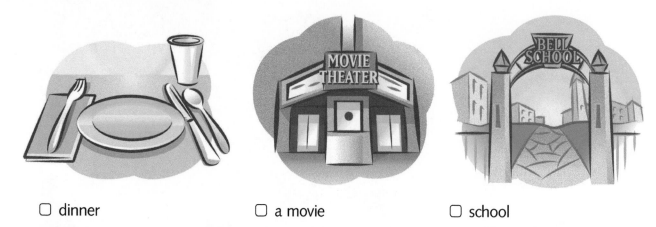

☐ dinner   ☐ a movie   ☐ school

Sometimes you don't need to understand everything you hear. You just want
the main idea, or general meaning.

DETAILS **B** 🎧 **Listen again. What are they going to eat? Check (✓) the correct answer.**

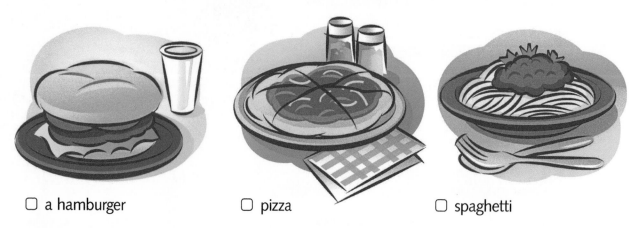

☐ a hamburger   ☐ pizza   ☐ spaghetti

Sometimes you only need to understand the details, or specific information.
Ask yourself, "What am I listening for?"

INFERENCE **C** 🎧 **Listen again. Will they go together? Check (✓) yes or no.**

☐ yes   ☐ no

Sometimes people don't say the exact words. You can still understand the meaning.
This is called listening "between the lines," or listening and making inferences.

Types of listening

Try it again. Two friends are talking on the telephone. Each time you listen, think about the information you need.

MAIN IDEA D Listen. What is the most important idea? Check (✓) the correct answer.

☐ going to the doctor   ☐ school

DETAILS E Listen again. What pages should she read? Write the page numbers.

_____ and _____

INFERENCE F Listen again. Did both students go to school today? Check (✓) *yes* or *no*.

☐ yes   ☐ no

You heard the same conversation three times. Each time, you listened for different reasons. Always think about why you are listening.

Meeting people

A Work with a partner. Complete the conversation with sentences from the box.

☑ Yes, I do. I love it.	☐ I really like pop music.
☐ Yes, I am. I'm studying art.	☐ I'm Sun Hee. It's nice to meet you, Brad.

Brad: Do you like jazz?

Sun Hee: *Yes, I do. I love it.*

How about you? What kind of music do you like?

Brad: _____

By the way, my name's Brad. I don't think we've met.

Sun Hee: _____

Brad: Nice to meet you, too. Are you a student?

Sun Hee: _____

B Imagine you are meeting someone for the first time. What questions would you ask? Complete questions 4 and 5. Then write your answers to all the questions.

1. What's your name? _____

2. Where are you from? _____

3. Are you a student? _____

4. Do you like _____? _____

5. What kind of _____ do you like? _____

C Work with a partner. Take turns asking and answering the questions from Exercise B.

How about you?

DETAILS **A** 🎧 **Listen. People are meeting at a party for the first time. What do they ask? Circle the correct answers.**

Kent and Lisa

1. (a.) How about you?
   b. How are you?

2. a. What kind of music do you like?
   b. Do you like this music?

3. a. What do you do?
   b. What's your name?

Lisa and Carlos

1. a. Are you a student?
   b. What are you studying?

2. a. Where do you study?
   b. What do you do?

3. a. Do you live here?
   b. Do you like living here?

4. a. Where are you from?
   b. Where are you going?

MAIN IDEA **B** 🎧 **Listen. Imagine you are talking to Lisa. What is your part of this conversation? Check (✓) your answers.**

1. ☑ Yes, I'm having fun, too.
   ☐ Yes, I do.

2. ☐ I am, too.
   ☐ I'm (*your name*).

3. ☐ Yes, my friends are here.
   ☐ I'm from (*your hometown*).

4. ☐ I study a lot.
   ☐ I'm a student.

5. ☐ Yes, I do.
   ☐ Yes, I am.

6. ☐ Yes, I do.
   ☐ I like jazz, too.

2 Around the world

DETAILS **A** 🎧 **Listen. There are many ways to greet people around the world. Match each greeting with two places.**

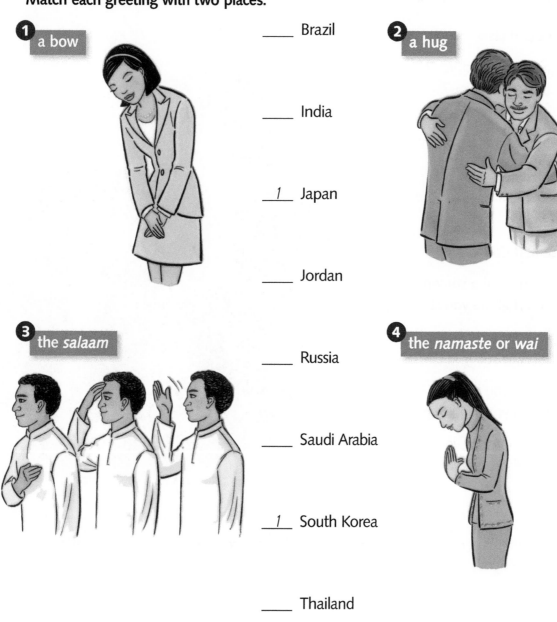

1 a bow

2 a hug

3 the *salaam*

4 the *namaste* or *wai*

_____ Brazil

_____ India

_1_ Japan

_____ Jordan

_____ Russia

_____ Saudi Arabia

_1_ South Korea

_____ Thailand

DETAILS **B** 🎧 **Listen again. Are the statements true or false? Check (✓) the correct answers.**

	true	false
1. In Japan and South Korea, people bow to show respect.	✓	☐
2. In Brazil, people usually kiss when they greet friends.	☐	☐
3. People often say "Health be with you" when they use the *salaam* in the Middle East.	☐	☐
4. The *namaste* or *wai* also means "Good morning."	☐	☐

SELF-STUDY *See page 84.*

Getting to know you

A What would you like to ask your classmates? Complete the survey questions. Use your own ideas.

PERSONAL SURVEY

Questions   **Names**

1. Do you _live near here_____?   _____

2. Are you _a university student_____?   _____

3. Do you _____?   _____

4. Are you _____?   _____

5. Do you _____?   _____

6. Are you _____?   _____

B **1.** Listen and practice. Notice the rising intonation of the questions.

Are you a university student?   Are you from Canada?

Do you study English?   Do you live near here?

2. Listen. Do you hear *Do you* or *Are you*? Check (✓) the correct answers.

	Do you	Are you		Do you	Are you		Do you	Are you
a.	✓	☐	c.	☐	☐	e.	☐	☐
b.	☐	☐	d.	☐	☐	f.	☐	☐

C Go around the class. Ask the questions from your Personal Survey in Exercise A. Who answers "yes"? Write the person's name.

Warming up

A Work with a partner. Label the picture with letters from the box.

a. aunt / nephew	d. father / daughter	g. husband / wife
b. brother / sister	e. grandfather / granddaughter	h. mother / son
c. cousins	f. grandmother / grandson	i. uncle / niece

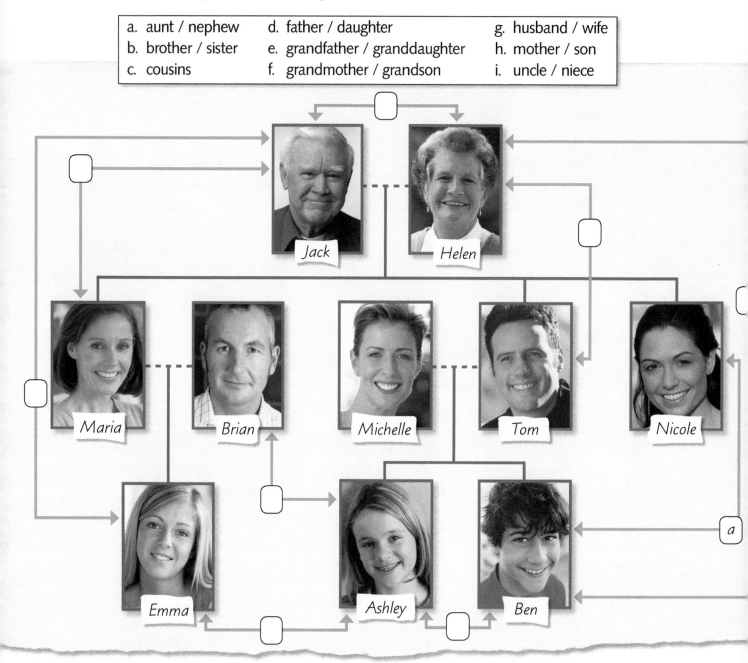

Jack   Helen

Maria   Brian   Michelle   Tom   Nicole

Emma   Ashley   Ben

a

B Close your books. Write as many words from Exercise A as you can on a separate piece of paper.

C Compare answers with your partner. Who wrote the most words?

Family photos

MAIN IDEA **A** 🎧 Listen. People are talking about their families. Who are they talking about? Check (✓) the correct pictures.

1. a ☑   b ☐

2. a ☐   b ☐

3. a ☐   b ☐

4. a ☐   b ☐

DETAILS **B** 🎧 Listen again. Circle the correct information.

1. The woman likes to take them to eat *hamburgers* / *(pizza)*

2. His parents live *nearby* / *far away.*

3. The picture was taken at her *niece's* / *mother's* birthday party.

4. The granddaughter *likes* / *doesn't like* school.

Family ties

A 🎧 **Listen. Jason is talking about his family. Circle the correct information.**

1. Morgan is Jason's *daughter* / *niece.*

2. Austin is Jason's *son* / *nephew.*

3. Nick is Jason's *brother* / *cousin.*

4. Frank is Jason's *uncle* / *father.*

5. Katherine is Jason's *wife* / *sister.*

6. Janice is Jason's *mother* / *aunt.*

DETAILS **B** 🎧 **Listen again. Are the statements true or false? Check (✓) the correct answers.**

	true	false
1. Morgan plays on a soccer team.	☑	☐
2. Morgan and Austin go to the same school.	☐	☐
3. Nick cooks a lot at home.	☐	☐
4. Frank doesn't like to cook much.	☐	☐
5. Katherine likes to read.	☐	☐
6. Janice and Frank often see their grandchildren.	☐	☐

SELF-STUDY *See page 85.*

My family

PREPARE **A** Think of a family member. Then complete the chart.

Name: Vinny	**Name:**
Relationship: cousin	**Relationship:**
Lives in: Singapore	**Lives in:**
Age: 23	**Age:**
Job or school: works in a music store	**Job or school:**
Interests: movies, volleyball, sleep	**Interests:**

PRACTICE **B** **1.** **Listen and practice. Notice the pronunciation of -s endings in verbs.**

-s = /s/	-s = /z/	-(e)s = /ɪz/
like → likes	go → goes	dance → dances
cook → cooks	live → lives	watch → watches
_____	_____	_____exercises_____
_____	_____	_____

2. **Write these words in the correct columns. Then listen and check your answers.**

✓exercises   plays   sleeps   studies   teaches   works

SPEAK **C** **1.** **Work with a partner. Talk about your family member from Exercise A.**

Let me tell you about my cousin.
   My cousin's name is Vinny. He lives in Singapore.
      He's 23 years old, and he works in a music store.
         He likes movies, plays volleyball, and sleeps a lot!

2. Join another pair. Tell them about your partner's family member.

Numbers

A Work with a partner. Take turns saying the numbers from 0 to 100.

●●●The Number Game●●●

0	1	2	3	4	5	6	7	8	9	10
11	12	13	14	15	16	17	18	19	20	
21	22	23	24	25	26	27	28	29	30	
31	32	33	34	35	36	37	38	39	40	
41	42	43	44	45	46	47	48	49	50	
51	52	53	54	55	56	57	58	59	60	
61	62	63	64	65	66	67	68	69	70	
71	72	73	74	75	76	77	78	79	80	
81	82	83	84	85	86	87	88	89	90	
91	92	93	94	95	96	97	98	99	100	

B What numbers are important for you? Write them on a separate piece of paper.

Your birthday	11/16/87 (month, day, year)	eleven, sixteen, eighty-seven
Your phone number	709-555-4236	seven-oh-nine, five-five-five, four-two-three-six
Another important number	07450	oh-seven-four-five-oh

C Play The Number Game with your partner. Take turns reading your numbers from Exercise B. Circle your partner's numbers on the game. Then check each other's games. Did you circle the correct numbers?

My birthday is 11/16/87.

On the phone

MAIN IDEA **A** Listen. People are calling for information. What places do they ask about? Check (✓) the correct places.

1 Sydney, Australia

☐ Sydney Hotel
☑ Park Hyatt

2 São Paulo, Brazil

☐ American Chamber of Commerce
☐ American Trade Office

3 Seoul, South Korea

☐ National Tourism Organization
☐ Central Tours Office

4 Toronto, Canada

☐ Blue Jays Baseball Team Ticket Office
☐ Maple Leafs Hockey Team Ticket Office

5 Tokyo, Japan

☐ United States Embassy
☐ American Center Library

6 Mexico City, Mexico

☐ Miami Airlines
☐ Colombia Airlines

DETAILS **B** Listen again. Write the phone numbers for the places.

1. _02-9241-1234_

2. _____

3. _____

4. _____

5. _____

6. _____

MAIN IDEA **A** 🎧 Listen. These teams are in a basketball tournament. Which team wins each game? Write the first letter of the team's name in the circles.

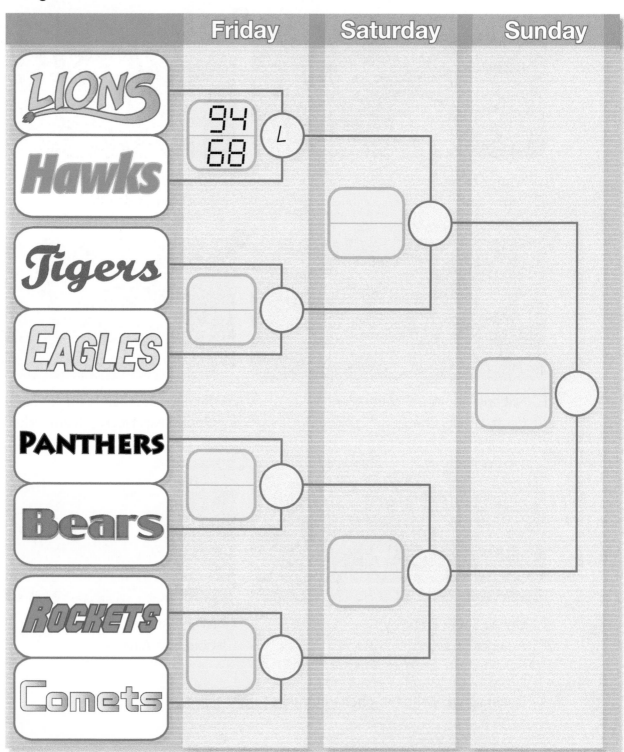

DETAILS **B** 🎧 Listen again. Write the score for each game in the chart.

Numbers, numbers

PREPARE **A** **Read the sentences. Circle one number in each sentence.**

1. His phone number is *555-3769 / 555-3679 / 555-3699*.

2. She is *13 / 30 / 17* years old.

3. The final score was *109 to 98 / 101 to 93 / 105 to 89*.

4. The hotel's phone number is *03-423-8164 / 03-422-8164 / 03-423-8964*.

5. The Lions lost to the Bears *30 to 13 / 40 to 14 / 50 to 15*.

6. His birthday is *9/5/94 / 5/9/94 / 9/5/74*.

PRACTICE **B** **1.** **Listen and practice. Notice the stress on the first syllable for numbers that end in *-ty*. Numbers that end in *-teen* have the stress on the last syllable.**

| twenty | thirty | forty | fifty |
| sixty | seventy | eighty | ninety |

| thirteen | fourteen | fifteen | sixteen |
| seventeen | eighteen | nineteen | |

2. **Listen. Which numbers are correct? Circle them.**

a. (13) 30   c. 14   40   e. 18   80

b. 17   70   d. 19   90   f. 16   60

SPEAK **C** **Work with a partner. Take turns reading your numbers from Exercise A. Draw a star (★) above the numbers you hear. Then check your answers. Who had the most correct numbers?**

His phone number is 555-3769.

Did you say 3679 or 3769?

Let's eat!

A Work with a partner. Label the picture with words from the box.

☑ beef	☐ cheese	☐ melons	☐ pasta
☐ bread	☐ chicken	☐ milk	☐ shrimp
☐ broccoli	☐ lemons	☐ mushrooms	☐ tomatoes

8.

9.

10.

7.

11.

6.

5.

12.

1. *beef*

2.

3.

4.

B Work with your partner. What other foods do you know? Write as many as you can. Then tell the class.

bananas

yogurt

What would you like?

A 🎧 Listen. People are ordering food in a restaurant. Check (✓) their orders.

1 soup

MENU
☐ Soup of the day
☑ French onion
☐ Vegetable

2 drink

Active Lemon Original
☐ Small
☐ Medium
☐ Large

3 toppings

Monster Burger
☐ cheese
☐ ketchup
☐ mustard
☐ onions
☐ lettuce
☐ pickles
☐ mushrooms
☐ tomatoes

4 salad

Lots to Toss
☐ garden salad
☐ pasta salad
☐ three bean salad

B 🎧 Listen again. Circle the correct information.

1. The woman doesn't like *vegetables* / *chicken*.

2. Active Lemon Light has *no flavor* / *too much sugar*.

3. The man thinks cheese *has too much fat* / *doesn't taste good*.

4. She doesn't like *onions* / *tomatoes*.

This looks great!

INFERENCE **A** Listen. Which foods are the people talking about? Number the pictures from 1 to 6. (There is one extra food item.)

DETAILS **B** Listen again. How did you know? Write the words that gave you the hints.

1. _dessert, chocolate, vanilla_

2. _____

3. _____

4. _____

5. _____

6. _____

SELF-STUDY *See page 87.*

The Food Game

PREPARE **A** Look at the game board. Think of at least one sentence for each topic.

My favorite home-cooked food is spaghetti.

START

| your favorite fast food | a food you hate | a food you can make | your favorite home-cooked food |

| the most unusual food you've eaten | a healthful food you often eat | your favorite snack | your favorite food when you were a child |

| your favorite restaurant | the best food for a hot day | your idea of a good breakfast | a foreign food you like | **FINISH** |

PRACTICE **B** **1.** Listen and practice. Notice the intonation of *Wh-* questions.

What's your favorite fast food?   What's a food you hate?

When do you eat dinner?   Where do you eat lunch?

2. Listen. Do you hear *What*, *When*, or *Where*? Check (✓) the correct answers.

	What	When	Where			What	When	Where
a.	✓	☐	☐		d.	☐	☐	☐
b.	☐	☐	☐		e.	☐	☐	☐
c.	☐	☐	☐		f.	☐	☐	☐

SPEAK **C** Play the game in Exercise A in groups of four. Put your markers on "Start."
Flip a coin to move.

 Move one space.

 Move two spaces.

heads   **tails**

When you land on a square, your classmates ask you questions about that topic.

Listening task 1 • Information

MAIN IDEA **A** 🎧 **Listen. People are talking about Thailand. What are the topics?
Circle the correct answers.**

1. a. vacations
   ⓑ greetings

2. a. houses
   b. people

3. a. families
   b. music

4. a. parties
   b. food

DETAILS **B** 🎧 **Listen again. Are the statements true or false? Check (✓) the correct answers.**

	true	false
1. Thais put their hands higher when they greet younger people.	☐	☑
2. About 11 percent of the people living in Thailand are Chinese.	☐	☐
3. Today, about 13 percent of Thais live in bigger families.	☐	☐
4. Thai dishes usually have a little meat or fish.	☐	☐

Listening task 2 • Food

DETAILS **A** 🎧 **Listen. A woman is talking about two popular dishes in Thailand. What is in each dish? Check (✓) the things. (There are two extra items for each dish.)**

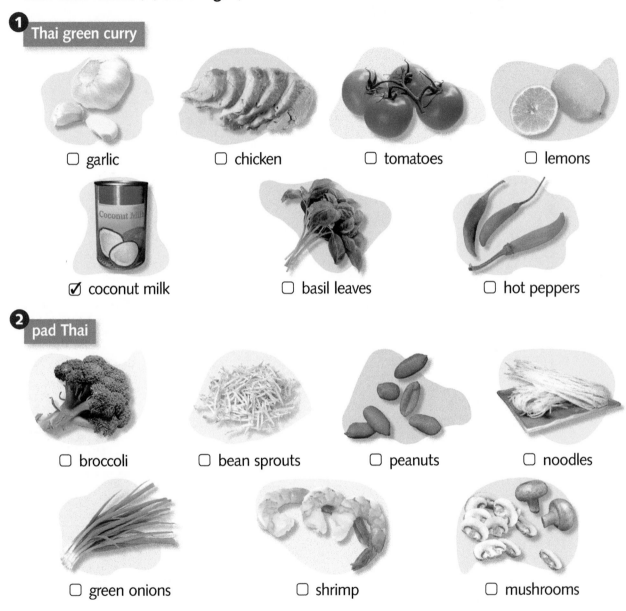

1 Thai green curry

☐ garlic ☐ chicken ☐ tomatoes ☐ lemons

☑ coconut milk ☐ basil leaves ☐ hot peppers

2 pad Thai

☐ broccoli ☐ bean sprouts ☐ peanuts ☐ noodles

☐ green onions ☐ shrimp ☐ mushrooms

DETAILS **B** 🎧 **Listen again. Circle the correct information.**

1. a. Thai people eat curry with *bread / rice.*
   b. The most popular Thai dish *is / is not* spicy.

2. a. The woman prefers pad Thai in *the U.S. / Thailand.*
   b. Thai dishes *are / are not* always spicy.

A What do you do in your free time? Complete the chart with *always, often, sometimes, hardly ever,* or *never.*

often   hardly ever

always   sometimes   never

How often do you . . . ?

1. go out for lunch   _hardly ever_

2. watch TV in the morning   _____

3. play sports in the afternoon   _____

4. go to a club on weekends   _____

5. visit relatives on vacation   _____

6. go to the movies on Saturday night   _____

B What other things do you do in your free time? Write as many as you can.
Then tell the class.

C Compare free-time activities with the class. Which activities are the most popular?
the least popular?

How often?

DETAILS **A** 🎧 Listen. People are talking about their free-time activities. How often do they do them? Write *always, often, sometimes, hardly ever*, or *never.*

1. He ___*hardly ever*___ plays sports in the afternoon.

2. She _____ goes to the movies on weekends.

3. He _____ watches TV at night.

4. She _____ goes to a club.

5. He _____ goes out for lunch.

6. She _____ visits relatives on Sunday.

DETAILS **B** 🎧 Listen again. Circle the reasons.

1. The man
   a. doesn't like to exercise.
   b. works in the afternoon.

2. The woman
   a. thinks movies are more exciting at the theater.
   b. doesn't have a DVD player.

3. The student
   a. likes many kinds of programs.
   b. doesn't have to study very much.

4. The woman thinks clubs
   a. are too expensive.
   b. aren't enjoyable.

5. The man likes
   a. to cook for friends.
   b. to go out for lunch with friends.

6. The woman likes to visit
   a. her grandparents.
   b. her cousins.

What's popular?

MAIN IDEA **A** 🎧 Listen. People in the U.S. spend their free time in the evening in different ways. Number the activities from 1 to 9.

Free-time activities	Percent
☐ reading	
☐ staying home with family	
☐ getting together with friends	
☐ resting or relaxing	
☐ eating out	
☐ playing a sport or exercising	
1 watching TV or DVDs	26%
☐ going to the movies or a play	
☐ other	

Source: *The Gallup Organization*

DETAILS **B** 🎧 Listen again. What percent of the people do each activity? Write the percents in the chart.

SELF-STUDY *See page 88.*

My free time

PREPARE **A** Think of activities you like doing and activities you don't like doing in each situation. Complete the chart.

	with friends	with my family	after class	on rainy days	alone
like	*shopping*				
don't like	*watching TV*				

PRACTICE **B** **1.** Listen and practice. Notice that the important words in the sentences are stressed.

I like shopping with friends.
I don't like going to the movies alone.

You like reading on rainy days.
Joe doesn't like staying home on weekends.

2. Circle the stressed words in the sentences. Then listen and check your answers.

a. On rainy (days), I like staying (home).
b. She likes playing sports with friends.
c. I don't like watching TV.

d. He doesn't like visiting relatives.
e. I like swimming after class.
f. You don't like studying alone.

SPEAK **C** Work in groups of three. Take turns sharing the activities you wrote in Exercise A. Can the group members guess the situation?

I like shopping, but I don't like watching TV.

I think you like shopping, but you don't like watching TV with your family.

Wrong. I like shopping, but I don't like watching TV with friends.

Great outfit!

A Work with a partner. Label the pictures with words from the box.

☑ blouse	☐ pants	☐ shorts	☐ suit
☐ cap	☐ sandals	☐ skirt	☐ sweater
☐ dress	☐ shirt	☐ sneakers	☐ T-shirt
☐ jacket	☐ shoes	☐ socks	☐ tie

1. _____
2. _____
3. _____
4. _____
5. blouse
6. _____
7. _____
8. _____
9. _____
10. _____
11. _____
12. _____
13. _____
14. _____
15. _____
16. _____

checks   solid   plaid   stripes

B What other clothing words do you know? Write as many as you can.

boots _____

C Work with your partner. Listen to your partner's words from Exercise B.
Write any new words above.

Choosing an outfit

MAIN IDEA **A** 🎧 Listen. Megan is telling her friend Erica what she's planning to wear to a party. Number the items from 1 to 6. (There are two extra items.)

INFERENCE **B** 🎧 Listen again. Does Erica like Megan's choices? Check (✓) the correct answers.

	likes	doesn't like		likes	doesn't like
1.	☐	☑	4.	☐	☐
2.	☐	☐	5.	☐	☐
3.	☐	☐	6.	☐	☐

The meaning of colors

MAIN IDEA **A** Listen. What do these colors mean for some people?
Match the colors with the words.

1. _e_ red   a. loyalty

2. ___ green   b. death

3. ___ yellow   c. looking thin

4. ___ black   d. happy feelings

5. ___ blue   e. power, strength, luck

6. ___ white   f. relaxation, nature

DETAILS **B** Listen again. Circle the correct information.

1. In China, you might see a red
   (dress)/ suit at a wedding.

2. Doctors in the U.S. often wear green
   shirts / jackets.

3. Yellow is a common color
   for girls' / babies' clothes.

4. If you want to look thin, wear
   stripes or checks / solid colors.

5. Blue is a good color to wear
   to a job / school interview.

6. In Nepal, the oldest daughter / son
   usually wears white for one year after
   a parent's death.

SELF-STUDY See page 89.

Find the differences.

PREPARE **A** Work with a partner. Student A, use this page. Student B, turn to page 78. Don't show your page to your classmates! Look carefully at what the people are wearing.

PRACTICE **B** **1.** Listen and practice. Notice the contractions for *is* and *is not*.

He's wearing sandals.   She's wearing a black skirt.
He isn't wearing a hat.   She isn't wearing a flowered shirt.

2. Listen. Do you hear the contraction for *is* or *is not*? Check (✓) the correct answers.

	is	is not		is	is not		is	is not
a.	☐	✓	c.	☐	☐	e.	☐	☐
b.	☐	☐	d.	☐	☐	f.	☐	☐

SPEAK **C** **1.** Talk about the pictures from Exercise A with your partner. Circle the differences in your picture.

> *In my picture, the father's wearing sandals.*

> *In my picture, he isn't wearing sandals. He's wearing shoes.*

2. How many differences did you find? Tell the class. Who found the most differences?

Warming up

A Label the pictures with words from the box.

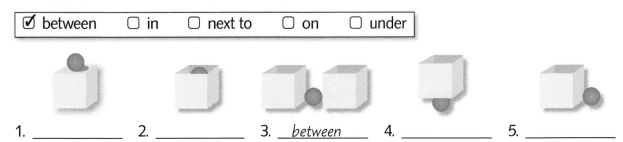

☑ between   ☐ in   ☐ next to   ☐ on   ☐ under

1. _____   2. _____   3. _between_   4. _____   5. _____

B Look at the picture for one minute. How many mistakes can you find?

ceiling

wall

floor

March

C Work with a partner. Cover the picture with a piece of paper. How many mistakes can you remember? Take turns making sentences with some of these words.

bookshelf	chair	couch	fishbowl	TV	vase
calendar	coffee table	curtains	rug	TV stand	windows

There's a calendar on the floor.   *The curtains are between the windows.*

Where does it go?

INFERENCE **A** 🎧 **Listen. Justin and Alex are roommates. Check (✓) the six things they are going to buy for their apartment.**

☐ chair   ☐ curtains   ☐ fishbowl   ☐ picture   ☐ radio
☑ couch   ☐ DVD player   ☐ lamp   ☐ plant   ☐ TV

DETAILS **B** 🎧 **Listen again. Where are they going to put the things? Number the picture from 1 to 6. (There is one extra space.)**

Listening task 2

Where's the heater?

MAIN IDEA **A** 🎧 How do people keep their houses warm in different countries?
Circle the heater in each room. Then listen and check your answers.

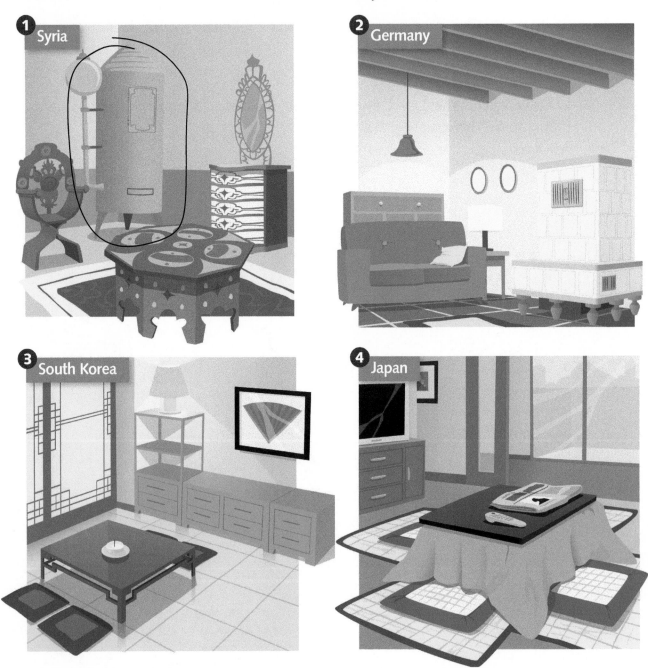

1 Syria

2 Germany

3 South Korea

4 Japan

DETAILS **B** 🎧 Listen again. Did the people visit or live in the countries?
Check (✓) the correct answers.

	visited	lived		visited	lived
1. Syria	☑	☐	3. South Korea	☐	☐
2. Germany	☐	☐	4. Japan	☐	☐

34 **Unit 7** In the house

SELF-STUDY *See page 90.*

My room

PREPARE **A** **What things are in your favorite room? Where are they? Draw a picture of the room.**

PRACTICE **B** **1.** 🎧 **Listen and practice. Notice the pronunciation of plural -s endings.**

-s = /s/	-s = /z/	-(e)s = /ɪz/
book → books	window → windows	vase → vases
lamp → lamps	chair → chairs	brush → brushes
_____	_bookshelves_	_____
_____	_____	_____

2. 🎧 **Write these words in the correct columns. Then listen and check your answers.**

✓ bookshelves*   curtains   dishes   glasses   photographs   plants

*singular: bookshelf

SPEAK **C** **Work with a partner. Take turns describing your rooms from Exercise A. Listen and draw your partner's room on a separate piece of paper. Then compare pictures.**

> _There are flowers on the table._
> _The bed is next to the wall._

Warming up

A Work with a partner. Match each sentence in the box with a sentence below that has the same meaning.

a. It's 2:00 P.M.	d. It's 6:00 A.M.	g. It's 8:30 A.M.
b. It's 10:15 P.M.	e. It's midnight.	h. It's noon.
c. It's 1:15. *or* It's a quarter after one.	f. It's 3:45. *or* It's a quarter to four.	i. It's 7:00 P.M.

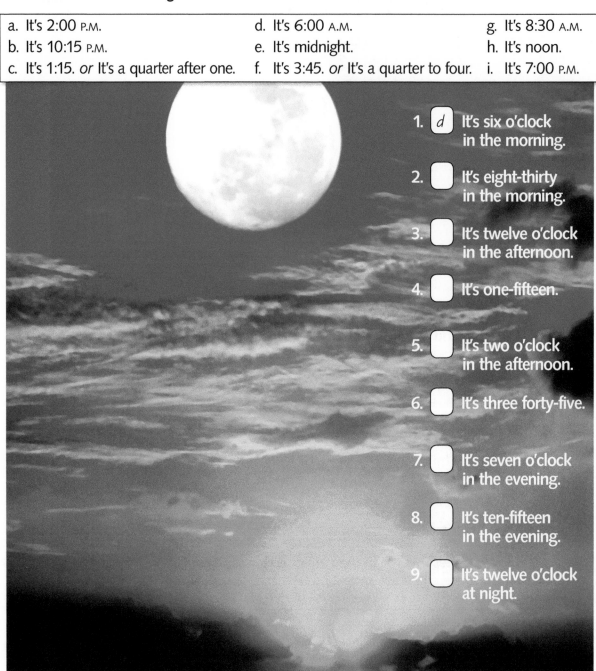

1. [d] It's six o'clock in the morning.

2. [ ] It's eight-thirty in the morning.

3. [ ] It's twelve o'clock in the afternoon.

4. [ ] It's one-fifteen.

5. [ ] It's two o'clock in the afternoon.

6. [ ] It's three forty-five.

7. [ ] It's seven o'clock in the evening.

8. [ ] It's ten-fifteen in the evening.

9. [ ] It's twelve o'clock at night.

B Say a time. Your partner says the same time another way. Then change roles.

It's six o'clock in the evening.   *It's 6:00 P.M.*

Changing plans

DETAILS **A** 🎧 **Listen. Some people are changing plans. Cross out the old information.
Write any new information.**

1

September

5
five

6
six
      6:15   Museum Café
Concert 7:30 ~~Hayes Hall~~
meet in front

7
seven

2

✈ FLIGHT DEPARTURES

FLIGHT	DESTINATION	DEPARTS	GATE
NA475	SEATTLE	4:25	12
NW723	TORONTO	4:45	7
CN305	SÃO PAOLO	6:00	5
CA39	TAIPEI	6:10	11

3

File	Date	12:37 p.m.

Lunch with Tony

   12:00 Bangkok Café

4

Monday	Tuesday	Wednesday
10:00	Math	
English test	homework	
	due	
4:00		
Soccer		

DETAILS **B** 🎧 **Listen again. Circle the correct reason for each change.**

1. ⓐ. They want to eat before the concert.
   b. They want to visit the museum.

2. a. The plane needs to be repaired.
   b. The weather is bad.

3. a. Bangkok Café will be crowded.
   b. Bangkok Café will be closed.

4. a. Professor Barton is sick.
   b. Daniel Smith is sick.

Time and cultures

MAIN IDEA **A** 🎧 **Listen. Some students are talking about time in different countries. Number the pictures from 1 to 4. (There is one extra picture.)**

DETAILS **B** 🎧 **Listen again. Circle the correct times.**

1. a. The invitations were for *7:00* / *7:30.*
   b. The guests came at *9:00* / *9:30.*

2. a. His professor said to come at *7:00* / *7:15.*
   b. He came at *7:10* / *7:30.*

3. a. The invitation was for *9:00* / *10:30.*
   b. The wedding started at *10:30* / *12:00.*

4. a. The next bus was at *10:17* / *10:18.*
   b. The bus left at *10:15* / *10:17.*

SELF-STUDY *See page 91.*

Making plans

PREPARE   **A**   **What do you want to do this weekend? Complete the chart with these activities or your own ideas.**

go to the movies   go to a concert   go out for lunch
          have a party   play or watch sports

	FRIDAY	SATURDAY	SUNDAY
Morning			
Afternoon			
Evening			

PRACTICE   **B**   **1.** **Listen and practice. Notice the pronunciation of *want to* and *have to*.**

want to = /wɑnə/	have to = /hæftə/

Do you want to go to a movie   Sure. I have to work until 6:00 P.M.
  on Saturday?   How about 7:00?

Do you want to go out on Friday?   I'm sorry. I can't. I have to work.

2. **Listen. Do you hear *want to* or *have to*? Check (✓) the correct answers.**

	want to	have to			want to	have to			want to	have to
a.	✓	☐		c.	☐	☐		e.	☐	☐
b.	☐	☐		d.	☐	☐		f.	☐	☐

SPEAK   **C**   **1. Work with a partner. Take turns inviting your partner to do the activities in your chart from Exercise A. Flip a coin to give your answers.**

   Say yes.
Decide the time.

   Say no.
Give a reason.

heads   **tails**

2. Now invite five different classmates to do the activities. How many times did people accept your invitation?

Listening task 1 • Information

MAIN IDEA **A** 🎧 Listen. People are talking about Kuwait. What are they talking about? Number the pictures from 1 to 4. (There is one extra picture.)

DETAILS **B** 🎧 Listen again. Circle the correct answers.

1. Kuwait is located between
   a. Iraq and Saudi Arabia.
   b. Iraq and Iran.

2. Shopping hours in Kuwait City start
   a. at 9:00 A.M.
   b. at 9:30 A.M.

3. Older gentlemen go to coffee shops
   a. in the afternoon.
   b. in the evening.

4. A traditional sport in Kuwait is
   a. horse racing.
   b. swimming.

Listening task 2 • Clothing styles

MAIN IDEA **A** 🎧 **Listen. A woman is describing women's clothing styles in Kuwait. Which style is she talking about? Check (✓) *Islamic, Western*, or *both*.**

Islamic style

hijab

abaya

Western style

	Islamic	Western	both			Islamic	Western	both
1.	☐	☐	☑	3.	☐	☐	☐
2.	☐	☐	☐	4.	☐	☐	☐

DETAILS **B** 🎧 **Listen again. Circle the correct information.**

1. In Kuwait, *45* / *⑤⑤* percent of the people come from other countries.

2. The *abaya* has wide *stripes* / *sleeves*.

3. Women enjoy wearing expensive scarves and *jewelry* / *jeans*.

4. It *is* / *isn't* common for a Kuwaiti woman to wear two styles on the same day.

Movies

A Work with a partner. What kinds of movies usually have these things?
Label the movies with words from the box.

☐ car chases	☐ good jokes	☑ romances	☐ singing
☐ dancing	☑ love stories	☐ scary scenes	☐ space travel
☐ fights	☐ robots	☐ silly situations	☐ vampires

METROLAND MOVIES

romance

love stories
romances

comedy

_____
_____

science fiction

_____
_____

action

_____
_____

musical

_____
_____

horror

_____
_____

B What other words do you know to talk about movies? Write as many as you can.

special effects
_____
_____
_____

C What kind of movie do you like best? What kind of movie does your
partner like best?

What's playing?

INFERENCE **A** 🎧 **Listen. What kinds of movies do you hear? Number the signs from 1 to 5. (There is one extra sign.)**

MAIN IDEA **B** 🎧 **Listen again. What's going on? Circle the correct information.**

1. Jessica *wants* / *doesn't want* Chris to go away.

2. The woman *is* / *is not* afraid.

3. They're having *an easy* / *a hard* time.

4. They're *going to* / *not going to* fight.

5. They *are chasing* / *caught* some robbers.

Film critics

INFERENCE **A** 🎧 Listen. What kinds of movies are the film critics talking about? Check (✓) the correct answers.

A NIGHT AT THE MOVIES

	Mark		Anna	
1. *Beyond the Moon* ☐ musical ☑ science fiction	😊	😞	😊	😞
2. *A Man's Best Friend* ☐ comedy ☐ romance	😊	😞	😊	😞
3. *San Francisco* ☐ musical ☐ romance	😊	😞	😊	😞
4. *Running* ☐ action ☐ comedy	😊	😞	😊	😞
5. *You and Me Alone* ☐ horror ☐ romance	😊	😞	😊	😞

INFERENCE **B** 🎧 Listen again. Do Mark and Anna like or dislike the movies? Circle the 😊 or the 😞.

SELF-STUDY *See page 92.*

My favorite movie

PREPARE **A** Complete these sentences about your favorite movie.

My favorite movie is _____ .

(movie title)

This movie is a _____ .

(kind of movie)

It's about _____ .

It stars _____ .

(actors' and actresses' names)

I like it because _____ .

PRACTICE **B** **1.** 🎧 Listen and practice. Notice the contractions for *is* and *are*.*

What's your favorite movie?   How's the acting?   Who's in it?
What're the special effects like?   How're the actors?   Who're the stars?

*These contractions are most common in spoken English.

2. 🎧 Listen. Do you hear the contraction for *is* or *are*? Check (✓) the correct answers.

	is	are			is	are			is	are
a.	✓	☐		c.	☐	☐		e.	☐	☐
b.	☐	☐		d.	☐	☐		f.	☐	☐

SPEAK **C** **1.** Work with a partner. Take turns asking and answering questions about your favorite movies. Use your sentences from Exercise A and the questions from Exercise B.

2. Complete the chart with information about your partner's favorite movie. Then tell the class about the movie.

_____ 's favorite movie is _____ .

(partner's name) (movie title)

This movie is a _____ .

(kind of movie)

It's about _____ .

It stars _____ .

(actors' and actresses' names)

He/She likes it because _____ .

Jenna's favorite movie is The Aviator. *This movie is a . . .*

Unit 9 Movies **45**

A typical day

Warming up

A What do you do on a typical day? Check (✓) your answers.

☐ check e-mail	☐ eat lunch	☐ have a cup of coffee	☐ study
☐ eat breakfast	☐ exercise	☐ listen to the radio	☐ take a bath or shower
☐ eat dinner	☐ go to school or work	☐ read the newspaper	☐ take a break

B Work with a partner. Take turns talking about your typical day. Use these words and your answers from Exercise A.

first	then	next	after that	finally

> *I get up at 6:30. First, I take a shower.*
> *Then I eat breakfast. Next, . . .*

What's your schedule?

MAIN IDEA **A** 🎧 Listen. Anne is looking for a roommate. She's asking Heather about her schedule. What are they talking about? Check (✓) the correct answers.

1. ☑ university classes
   ☐ a part-time job

2. ☐ breakfast
   ☐ lunch

3. ☐ classes
   ☐ exercising

4. ☐ a restaurant
   ☐ the library

5. ☐ dinner
   ☐ friends

6. ☐ pets
   ☐ evenings

DETAILS **B** 🎧 Listen again. Circle the correct answers.

1. Heather gets up
   a. before 8:00 A.M.
   b. at 8:00 A.M.

2. Heather eats breakfast
   a. at home.
   b. at school.

3. Heather exercises
   a. at the sports center.
   b. at the gym.

4. Heather uses the computer
   a. to look for information.
   b. to check e-mail.

5. Heather likes to cook
   a. Italian food.
   b. Mexican food.

6. Heather doesn't go out because
   a. she doesn't have enough money.
   b. she doesn't have enough time or energy.

Daily schedules

MAIN IDEA **A** 🎧 Listen. People are talking about their daily schedules. Check (✓) the three activities each person mentions.

1 Alex Chan, office worker, Taipei

- ☐ drinks tea   ☐ checks e-mail
- ☐ exercises   ☐ eats lunch

2 Sophie Martin, student, Paris

- ☐ eats breakfast   ☐ meets friends
- ☐ exercises   ☐ watches TV

3 Hannah Williams, server, Vancouver

- ☐ cleans   ☐ listens to the radio
- ☐ takes a break   ☐ takes the bus home

4 Emilio Maisano, store clerk, Rome

- ☐ goes to work   ☐ meets friends
- ☐ eats lunch   ☐ plays soccer

DETAILS **B** 🎧 Listen again. Write the correct times.

1. a. Alex leaves his house at _____ .
   b. He starts work at _____ .
   c. He finishes work at _____ .

2. a. Sophie sleeps until _____ or _____ .
   b. She has a piano lesson at _____ .
   c. She gets home around _____ .

3. a. Hannah goes to work at _____ .
   b. She takes a break around _____ .
   c. She works until _____ .

4. a. Emilio eats breakfast at _____ .
   b. He eats lunch from _____ to _____
   c. He leaves work at _____ .

SELF-STUDY *See page 93.*

The perfect schedule

PREPARE **A** **What is the perfect schedule for you? Write at least four activities and the times in the chart.**

Activity	Time
wake up	*10:00 A.M.*

PRACTICE **B** **1.** 🎧 **Listen and practice. Notice the linked sounds of consonants and vowels.**

Mia gets up at eight.   Next, she exercises at the sports center.

Then she has a cup of coffee.   Finally, she arrives at work and checks e-mail.

2. 🎧 **Draw lines for the linked sounds. Then listen and check your answers.**

a. John works until five.

b. He sometimes goes out for dinner.

c. Then he takes a bus home.

d. Rita wakes up at eleven.

e. Then she drinks a cup of tea.

f. She uses a computer at work.

SPEAK **C** **1. Work with a partner. Take turns talking about your perfect schedules.**

What's your perfect schedule like?

I get up every day at 10:00 A.M.

Really? I always get up at 10:00 A.M.

2. Tell the class about your partner's schedule.

Naomi gets up at 10:00 A.M. Next, . . .

A Work with a partner. Use the map to answer the questions. Check your answers on page 79.

1. What's **across from** the restaurant?
2. What's **between** the movie theater and the aquarium?
3. What's **next to** the bank?
4. What's **around the corner from** the toy store?
5. What's next to the pet store **on the right**?
6. What's next to the entrance **on the left**?

B Label the pictures with phrases from the box.

☐ go across   ☐ go straight   ☐ turn left   ☐ turn right

1. _____   2. _____   3. _____   4. _____

C Work with your partner. Start at the entrance on the map. Take turns giving directions to a location. Guess the place.

Go straight. Turn left at the food court. It's across from the restaurant.

Is it the tower?

Where is it?

MAIN IDEA

A 🎧 Listen. Where are the places? Number the map from 1 to 6. (There is one extra place.)

1. Monkey Mountain
2. Lion Land
3. Children's Zoo
4. Ice House
5. Brazilian Rain Forest
6. Life Science Center

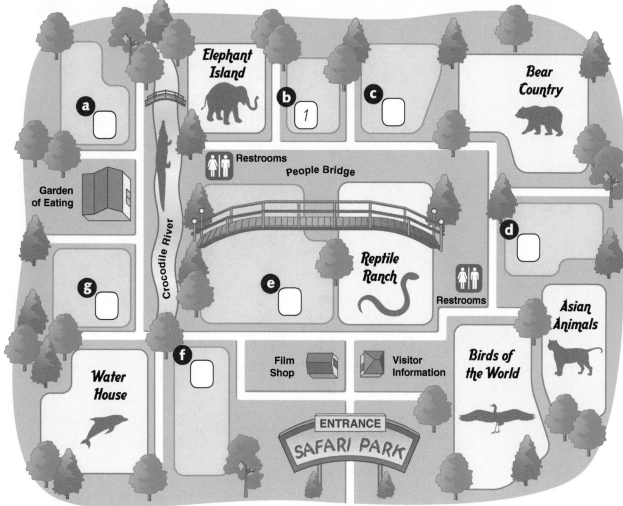

INFERENCE

B 🎧 Listen again. Who wants to see these things? Check (✓) *boy*, *girl*, or *both*.

	boy	girl	both
1. monkeys			✓
2. lions			
3. rabbits and sheep			
4. penguins			
5. insects			
6. souvenirs			

Listening task 2

Find the treasure.

A 🎧 **Listen. A boy is playing a video game. Where is he? Number the places from 1 to 6. (There are three extra places.)**

B 🎧 **Listen again. Circle the correct information.**

1. The *boy* / *girl* has played the game a lot.

2. The bag has *money* / *rocks*.

3. The boy buys *a sandwich* / *an ice cream cone*.

4. The boy gives the man *a ticket* / *the ice cream cone*.

5. The monkey gives the boy a *map* / *key*.

6. The *map* / *treasure* is behind the door.

SELF-STUDY *See page 94.*

Map it!

A Draw a map from your school to a place nearby on a separate piece of paper. Then write simple directions. Don't show your map to your classmates!

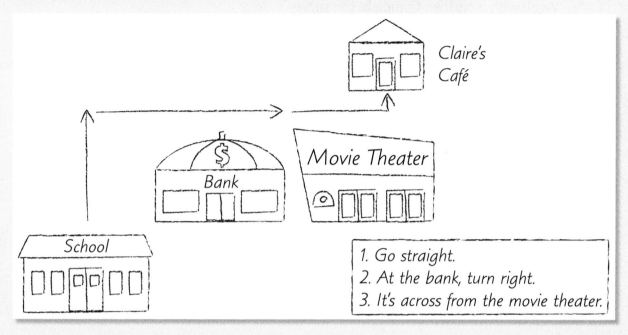

Claire's Café

Movie Theater

Bank

School

1. Go straight.
2. At the bank, turn right.
3. It's across from the movie theater.

B **1.** Listen and practice. Notice the stress for clarification.

Did you say turn right or left? Turn right.
Should I go straight or turn left? Go straight.
Is it next to the café or behind the café? It's next to the café.

2. Circle the stressed words in the sentences. Then listen and check your answers.

a. Is the restroom (across) from the café or (next) to it?

b. What's next to the movie theater, the aquarium or the bank?

c. Do I go straight or turn right at the bridge?

d. Is the restroom around the corner from the café or the aquarium?

e. Is the entrance on the left or the right of the food court?

C Work in groups of three. Student A, give directions to your place in Exercise A. Students B and C, guess the place.

Start at the main gate of the school. Go straight. At the bank, turn . . .

A Work with a partner. Complete the survey.

GIFT SURVEY

◆◆◆ — *What kinds of gifts do you give when . . . ?*

1. you go to a friend's wedding
   _money_____ _____

2. you visit a friend in another country
   _____ _____

3. you celebrate a friend's birthday
   _____ _____

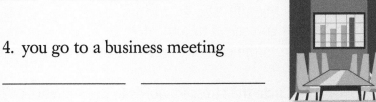

4. you go to a business meeting
   _____ _____

5. you want to give something to someone you love
   _____ _____

B What gifts in your culture can have a bad meaning? Write as many as you can. Then compare answers with the class.

Gift-giving occasions

MAIN IDEA **A** 🎧 **Listen. What are the gift-giving occasions? Number the occasions from 1 to 6. (There are two extra occasions.)**

____ anniversary   ____ business meeting   ____ graduation   _1_ retirement
____ birthday   ____ Father's Day   ____ Mother's Day ____ thank you

INFERENCE **B** 🎧 **Listen again. Which gifts are the people going to buy? Check (✓) the correct pictures.**

1

a. ☑   b. ☐

2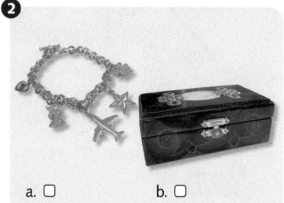

a. ☐   b. ☐

3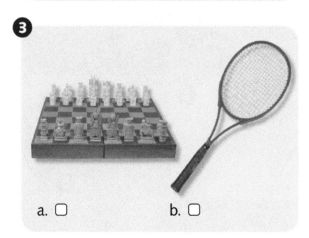

a. ☐   b. ☐

4

a. ☐   b. ☐

5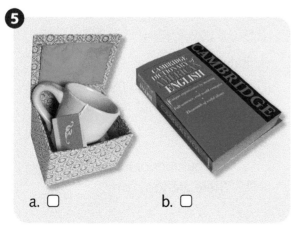

a. ☐   b. ☐

6

a. ☐   b. ☐

Gifts and cultures

MAIN IDEA
A 🎧 Listen. Sometimes the meanings of gifts are different among cultures. Cross out (*X*) the items that are not good gifts.

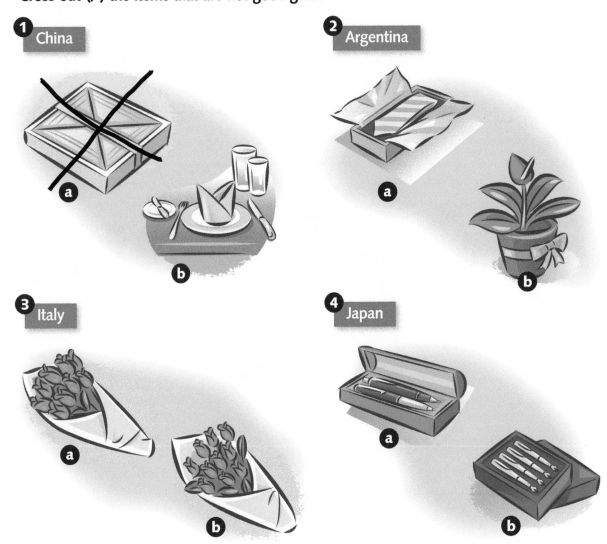

1 China

2 Argentina

3 Italy

4 Japan

DETAILS
B 🎧 Listen again. Why are the items not good gifts?
Circle the correct answers.

1. China
   a. It can also mean "Good-bye."
   b. It's too cheap.

2. Argentina
   a. It's too personal.
   b. It isn't comfortable.

3. Italy
   a. They're too expensive.
   b. The number of roses is unlucky.

4. Japan
   a. The number of items is unlucky.
   b. There are too many.

SELF-STUDY *See page 95.*

Gift exchange

PREPARE **A** Choose five classmates. Think of an occasion to give each one a gift. Complete the chart.

Classmate's name	Occasion	Gift
Sam	birthday	chocolate

PRACTICE **B** **1.** 🎧 Listen and practice. Notice the intonation and pause before names.

These flowers are for you, Maria.   Oh, thanks, Mieko. They're beautiful.

Congratulations on your new job, Susan.   Oh, this is lovely, John! Thank you so much!

2. 🎧 Listen. Does the speaker say the person's name? Check (✓) *yes* or *no*.

	yes	no		yes	no		yes	no
a.	☐	✓	c.	☐	☐	e.	☐	☐
b.	☐	☐	d.	☐	☐	f.	☐	☐

SPEAK **C** Go around the class. Imagine you are giving your gifts to the classmates in Exercise A. Practice using your classmates' names.

> Happy birthday, Sam.
> This chocolate is for you.

> Thank you, Sara.
> I love chocolate!

Listening task 1 • Information

MAIN IDEA **A** 🎧 **Listen. People are talking about Italy. Which cities are they talking about? Number the pictures from 1 to 4. (There is one extra picture.)**

Milan

Venice

Rome

1

Florence

Bologna

DETAILS **B** 🎧 **Listen again. There is one mistake in each sentence. Cross out the incorrect words. Then write the correct information.**

1. Italy is most famous for its romance and ~~horror~~ *comedy* movies.

2. This city is the best place to see the newest car designs.

3. In this city, the Boboli Gardens are next to the Pitti Palace.

4. The pasta sauce from this city has meat and mushrooms.

Listening task 2 • University life

MAIN IDEA **A** 🎧 **Listen. An Italian student is talking about university life in the U.S. and Italy. What is he talking about? Check (✓) the topics. (There are two extra topics.)**

- ☐ birthday gifts
- ☐ free-time activities
- ☐ graduation
- ☐ housing
- ☐ school schedules
- ☐ a typical school day

DETAILS **B** 🎧 **Listen again. Where are these statements true? Check (✓) *in Italy, in the U.S.,* or *in both*.**

Students	in Italy	in the U.S.	in both
1. have three months for summer vacation			
2. eat lunch in the university cafeteria			
3. meet for coffee in their free time			
4. usually live at home with their parents			

Part-time jobs

A Work with a partner. Label the pictures with words from the box.

☑ childcare worker	☐ convenience store clerk	☐ porter	☐ tour guide
☐ cleaning staff	☐ lifeguard	☐ server	☐ tutor

Part-time jobs for students

childcare worker

B Work with your partner. What other part-time jobs do you know? Write as many as you can.

C Now change partners. Take turns reading your words from Exercise B. Write any new words above.

What's the job?

INFERENCE **A** 🎧 **Listen. Who are the people below talking to? Write the other people's jobs. (There is one extra job.)**

☐ a childcare worker	☐ a lifeguard	☐ a server	☑ a tutor
☐ a convenience store clerk	☐ a porter	☐ a tour guide	

1

2

3

a tutor _____

_____

_____

4

5

6

_____

_____

_____

DETAILS **B** 🎧 **Listen again. Circle the correct information.**

1. The student has to write a (_five-page_)/ _ten-page_ paper.

2. They're going to drink _coffee_ / _tea_.

3. The woman is buying a _newspaper_ / _magazine_.

4. They're in room _726_ / _627_.

5. The man wants to send a picture to his _cousin_ / _sister_.

6. Michael is a bit _tired_ / _hungry_.

DETAILS **A** 🎧 **Listen. People are interviewing for jobs. Check (✓) the correct information about each job below.**

1 park ranger

2 camp counselor

3 business intern

4 tennis instructor

	experience required	no experience required	full-time	part-time	paid	volunteer
1.	✓	☐	☐	✓	☐	✓
2.	☐	☐	☐	☐	☐	☐
3.	☐	☐	☐	☐	☐	☐
4.	☐	☐	☐	☐	☐	☐

INFERENCE **B** 🎧 **Listen again. Will the people accept the jobs? Check (✓) *yes* or *no*.**

	yes	no			yes	no
1.	☐	☐		3.	☐	☐
2.	☐	☐		4.	☐	☐

SELF-STUDY *See page 96.*

My ideal job

PREPARE **A** **What is very important to you in a job? What doesn't matter?**
Rank each job feature with a symbol (★ or O).

Job features

☆ = It's very important.   O = It doesn't matter.

___ work alone	___ wear a uniform	___ do something different every day
___ work with people	___ work inside	___ have the same routine
___ work with children	___ work outside	___ have a lot of responsibility
___ work part-time	___ work in an office	___ have little responsibility
___ work full-time	___ volunteer	___ have a high salary

PRACTICE **B** **1.** 🎧 **Listen and practice. Notice the stressed syllables.**

lifeguard	assistant	volunteer
uniform	experience	routine

2. 🎧 **Listen. Circle the stressed syllables.**

a. intern   c. salary   e. convenience
b. instructor   d. outdoors   f. alone

SPEAK **C** **1. Work with a partner. Take turns asking and answering questions**
about the job features in Exercise A.

Do you want to work alone?

Yes, I do. It's very important to me.
OR
No, I don't. It doesn't matter to me.

2. Join another pair. What jobs would be good for your partner?
Tell your classmates.

I think Shu-ling would be a good tennis instructor.
She wants to work outside.

A Work with a partner. When do people do these things? Write a holiday or celebration for the activities in the box.

do a special dance _____	go to a parade _____
eat special food _____	ring bells _____
fly special flags _____	watch fireworks _____
give presents _____	wear special clothes _____

B Work with your partner. What other holidays and celebrations do you know? Write as many as you can.

Fireworks, food, and fun

DETAILS **A** 🎧 **Listen. When are these celebrations? Write the celebrations in the correct months.**

1. St. Patrick's Day
2. Moon Festival
3. Bob Marley Day
4. Day of the Dead
5. Kartini Day
6. St. Lucia's Day

JANUARY	FEBRUARY	MARCH	APRIL
_____	_____	St. Patrick's Day	_____
MAY	JUNE	JULY	AUGUST
_____	_____	_____	_____
SEPTEMBER	OCTOBER	NOVEMBER	DECEMBER
_____	_____	_____	_____

DETAILS **B** 🎧 **Listen again. What do people do to celebrate? Match each celebration with an activity.**

1. ____ St. Patrick's Day
2. ____ Moon Festival
3. ____ Bob Marley Day
4. ____ Day of the Dead
5. ____ Kartini Day
6. ____ St. Lucia's Day

a. visit graves
b. go to concerts
c. share special lunches
d. wear special clothes
e. go to a parade
f. eat special cakes

Celebration time

MAIN IDEA **A** 🎧 Listen. People are describing celebrations around the world. Number the pictures from 1 to 4.

Water festival

Carnaval

Chinese New Year

Kite-flying festival

DETAILS **B** 🎧 Listen again. Circle the correct information.

1. Cutting strings *brings good fortune / takes away bad luck.*

2. Pouring water *shows respect / symbolizes a long life.*

3. The purpose of this holiday is *to teach the samba / for people to have a good time.*

4. It's important to start the year *without owing money / with lots of money.*

SELF-STUDY *See page 97.*

Holiday memories

PREPARE **A** Check (✓) three holidays you want to talk about.

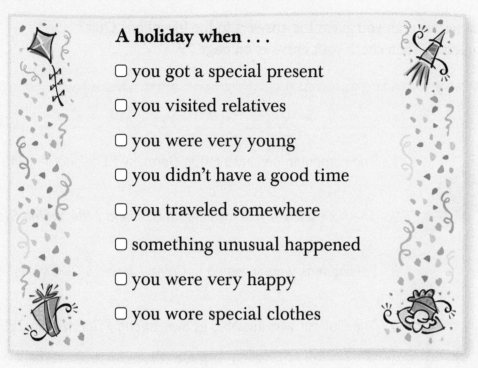

A holiday when . . .

☐ you got a special present

☐ you visited relatives

☐ you were very young

☐ you didn't have a good time

☐ you traveled somewhere

☐ something unusual happened

☐ you were very happy

☐ you wore special clothes

PRACTICE **B** **1.** 🎧 Listen and practice. Notice the pronunciation of *Did you* and *What did you*.

Did you = /dɪdʒə/	What did you = /wʌt dɪdʒə/

Did you give presents?   What did you buy?
Did you wear special clothes?   What did you do?

2. 🎧 Listen. Do you hear *Did you* or *What did you*? Check (✓) the correct answers.

	Did you	What did you		Did you	What did you		Did you	What did you
a.	☐	☑	c.	☐	☐	e.	☐	☐
b.	☐	☐	d.	☐	☐	f.	☐	☐

SPEAK **C** Work in groups of three. Talk about your holidays from Exercise A. Ask at least one question about each classmate's holiday.

One holiday, we visited my grandparents in Mexico.

Really? What did you do there?

Inventions

A Work with a partner. Can you guess the answers to the Inventions Quiz?
Circle your guesses. Then check your answers on page 79.

INVENTIONS QUIZ

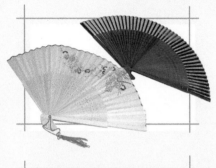

1. The computer was invented in *Germany / England* in 1943.

2. The fax machine was invented in *Scotland / the United States*.

3. Folding fans were invented in *China / Japan* 1,200 years ago.

4. The first car was invented in *Switzerland / Germany* in 1885.

5. Chocolate bars were invented in *England / Colombia* in the 1800s.

6. The first accurate calendar came from *Mexico / England*.

7. The mechanical clock was invented in *China / Switzerland* in 725.

8. Puppets probably came from *India / South America*.

B What inventions could you not live without? Write as many as you can.

microwave oven

C Compare answers from Exercise B with the class. Which inventions are
the most popular?

What's the invention?

INFERENCE **A** 🎧 Listen. What are the people talking about? Number the pictures from 1 to 6. (There are two extra pictures.)

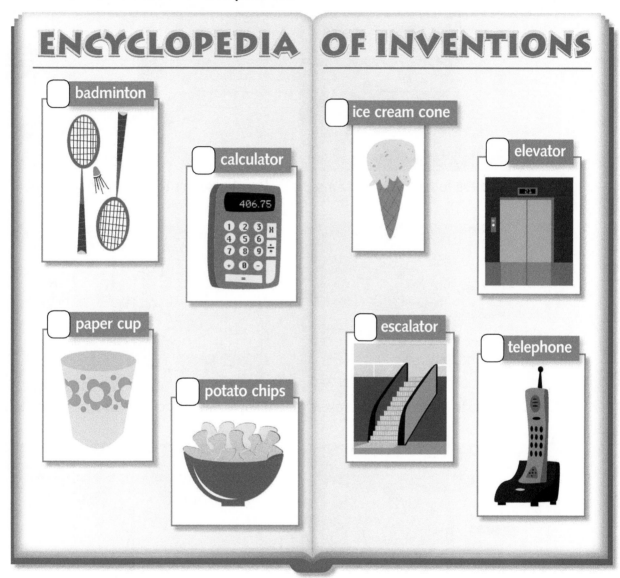

ENCYCLOPEDIA OF INVENTIONS

- badminton
- calculator
- paper cup
- potato chips
- ice cream cone
- elevator
- escalator
- telephone

DETAILS **B** 🎧 Listen again. Circle the reasons for the inventions.

1. a. It was a children's game.
   b. It was a fortune-telling game.

2. a. They were a joke.
   b. A customer wanted fast food.

3. a. It was made for tall buildings.
   b. It was made for a king.

4. a. There were no more cups.
   b. People wanted to eat while they walked.

5. a. People wanted to take drinks home.
   b. A rich man didn't want to get sick.

6. a. The inventor wanted to work faster.
   b. The inventor wanted to help his father.

MAIN IDEA **A** 🎧 **Listen. What are these things used for? Circle the correct information.**

1

People use these to block *the sun / insects.*

2

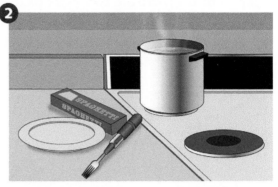

People use this to *eat / cook* spaghetti.

3

Cats use these to *clean the floor / exercise.*

4

People use this to *exercise / sit* on the train.

5

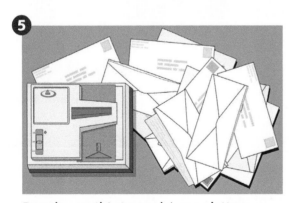

People use this to *seal / open* letters.

6

People use this to *cover / hold* their cameras.

INFERENCE **B** 🎧 **Listen again. Will the people buy the products? Check (✓) *yes* or *no.***

	yes	no		yes	no		yes	no
1.	☐	☐	3.	☐	☐	5.	☐	☐
2.	☐	☐	4.	☐	☐	6.	☐	☐

SELF-STUDY *See page 98.*

Thank you, Mr. Robot!

PREPARE **A** Work with a partner. Imagine you have a robot that can do five chores. What chores can your robot do? You can add your own ideas. Check (✓) the chores.

- ☐ clean the bathroom
- ☐ cook
- ☐ do the dishes
- ☐ do the laundry
- ☐ dust
- ☐ make the bed
- ☐ vacuum
- ☐ water the plants
- ☐ _____
  (your own idea)
- ☐ _____
  (your own idea)

PRACTICE **B** **1.** Listen and practice. Notice the pronunciation of *can* and *can't*.

can = /kən/	can't = /kænt/

My robot can vacuum.   My robot can't vacuum, but it can dust.
Can your robot do the dishes? No, it can't. It can't do the dishes.

2. Listen. Do you hear *can* or *can't*? Check (✓) the correct answers.

	can	can't			can	can't			can	can't
a.	✓	☐		c.	☐	☐		e.	☐	☐
b.	☐	☐		d.	☐	☐		f.	☐	☐

SPEAK **C** **1.** Work with your partner from Exercise A. Join another pair. Take turns asking and answering questions about your robots.

Can your robot dust?

No, it can't, but it can do the dishes.

2. Tell the class about your robots. Which robot is the most useful? the most unusual? the silliest?

Warming up

A Work with a partner. Label the pictures with words from the box.

☑ diamonds	☐ genie	☐ money	☐ stonecutter
☐ farmer	☐ gold	☐ prince	☐ stones
☐ field	☐ magic lamp	☐ rich man	☐ wheat

The Farmer and His Sons

1.
2.
3. *diamonds*
4.
5.
6.

THE STONECUTTER

1.
2.
3.
4.
5.
6.

B Write the words from Exercise A in the correct columns.

Kinds of treasure	Magical things	People	Nature
diamonds			

C Work with your partner. What other words do you know? Write any new words above.

The farmer and his sons

MAIN IDEA **A** 🎧 **Listen. You will hear a traditional folktale. Number the pictures from 1 to 6.**

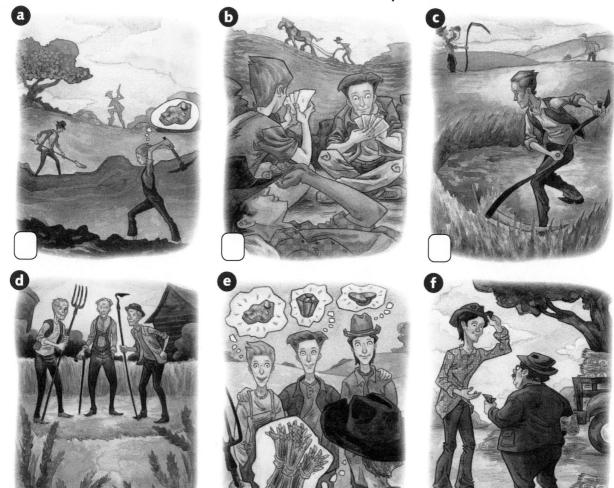

DETAILS **B** 🎧 **Listen again. Circle the correct answers.**

1. The three sons lived
   a. with their father.
   b. by themselves.

2. The sons were most interested in
   a. farming.
   b. treasure.

3. The sons dug up the field
   a. to find treasure.
   b. to plant wheat.

4. The fields were full of
   a. treasure.
   b. wheat.

5. The sons sold
   a. the farm.
   b. the wheat.

6. Their father's treasure was
   a. the land.
   b. gold.

The stonecutter

MAIN IDEA **A** Listen to the story of the stonecutter. What is the main idea of each part of the story? Number the statements from 1 to 4.

_____ The stonecutter was too busy, and he was tired.
He asked the genie to make him a rich man.

_____ The stonecutter saw a man building a stone house.
He understood that he didn't need money and power to be happy.

_____ The stonecutter lived with his wife in a small house.
They were poor but happy.

_____ The stonecutter found a genie in a magic lamp.
He asked the genie to make him a prince.

INFERENCE **B** Listen again. Which statements are probably true? Check (✓) the correct answers.

1. ☐ The stonecutter wanted to change his job.
   ☐ The stonecutter did not want to change his job.

2. ☐ The stonecutter wanted to have more money.
   ☐ The stonecutter wanted to be more handsome.

3. ☐ The prince and his wife wanted to be alone.
   ☐ The prince and his wife were happy to have visitors.

4. ☐ The story means money is important.
   ☐ The story means happiness is important.

SELF-STUDY *See page 99.*

Once upon a time . . .

PREPARE **A** Work with a partner. Complete the sentences. Then number the sentences in order to make a story.

The boy lived in _____ .
(place)

Once upon a time, there was a young boy.   *1*

One day, the boy met _____ .
(a magic person)

The boy said, "I want _____ ."
(thing)

_____ said, "What is your wish?"
(the same magic person)

_____ gave the boy _____ .
(the same magic person)   (thing)

PRACTICE **B** **1.** Listen and practice. Notice the pause after a comma when telling a story.

Once upon a time, [pause] there was a young boy.
One day, [pause] the boy met a princess.
He said, [pause] "I want to be a prince."
When the princess smiled, [pause] he became a prince.

2. Add a comma to show the pause in each sentence. Then listen and check your answers.

a. One day, a young boy was working in the field.

b. The boy was poor so he worked very hard.

c. When the boy finished working a genie came and spoke to him.

d. Because the boy worked so hard the genie gave him three wishes.

SPEAK **C** Work in groups of four. Take turns telling your stories. Ask and answer questions about your classmates' stories.

Once upon a time, there was a young boy.

What was his name?

Listening task 1 • Information

MAIN IDEA **A** 🎧 **Listen. People are talking about India. What are the topics? Check (✓) the correct answers.**

1. ☐ languages   ☐ the location   ☐ the weather
2. ☐ restaurants   ☐ food and drinks   ☐ shopping
3. ☐ a scientist and inventor   ☐ a movie star   ☐ a teacher
4. ☐ music   ☐ sports   ☐ movies

DETAILS **B** 🎧 **Listen again. Circle the correct answers.**

1. India has
   a. two national languages.
   b. twenty-two national languages.

2. Many Indians don't eat
   a. beef.
   b. mangoes.

3. Aryabhatta invented
   a. the number zero.
   b. the soccer ball.

4. Indian movies often show
   a. special effects and good jokes.
   b. fighting and dancing.

Listening task 2 • A festival

MAIN IDEA **A** 🎧 **Listen. A woman is telling the story of the Indian festival Diwali. Number the sentences in the correct order from 1 to 7.**

_____ She kept him awake all night.

_____ She lit many candles and lights.

_____ Her husband was saved.

_1_ There was a woman who tried to save her husband's life by keeping away the lord of death.

_____ When the lord of death came to take her husband, the lord was blinded by the lights.

_____ She put her jewelry all over the house.

_7_ The story explains the significance of the lights and why Diwali is celebrated.

DETAILS **B** 🎧 **Listen. How do people celebrate Diwali today? Check (✓) five things they do.**

☐ buy new clothes ☐ give presents ☐ ring bells
☐ dance ☐ go to a parade ☐ set off fireworks
☐ eat special food ☐ meet relatives ☐ visit graves

Appendix

PREPARE **A** Work with a partner. Student B, use this page. Don't show your page to your classmates! Look carefully at what the people are wearing.

PRACTICE **B** **1.** 🎧 Listen and practice. Notice the contractions for *is* and *is not*.

He's wearing sandals.   She's wearing a black skirt.
He isn't wearing a hat.   She isn't wearing a flowered shirt.

2. 🎧 Listen. Do you hear the contraction for *is* or *is not*? Check (✓) the correct answers.

	is	is not		is	is not		is	is not
a.	☐	☑	c.	☐	☐	e.	☐	☐
b.	☐	☐	d.	☐	☐	f.	☐	☐

SPEAK **C** **1.** Talk about the pictures from Exercise A with your partner. Circle the differences in your picture.

> In my picture, the father's wearing sandals.

> In my picture, he isn't wearing sandals. He's wearing shoes.

2. How many differences did you find? Tell the class. Who found the most differences?

Answer key

Unit 11 Locations
Page 50
Warming up
Exercise A
1. the tower
2. the Internet café
3. the pet store
4. the movie theater, the tower
5. the arcade
6. the restaurant

Unit 15 Inventions
Page 68
Warming up
Exercise A
1. England
2. Scotland
3. Japan
4. Germany
5. England
6. Mexico
7. China
8. India

Activation

A speaking and listening game

- Work in groups of four.
- Put a marker on "Start."
- Close your eyes. Touch the "How many spaces?" box with a pencil. Move that many spaces.
- Follow the instructions.
- Take turns.

Where can you hear, read, or use English outside this class? How many places can you think of in two minutes?

Describe a piece of clothing you bought recently.

Are you usually early, on time, or late for events? Give some examples.

What is your favorite restaurant? Give directions to it.

Start

Finish

Describe a perfect day. What activities would you do?

Name a story that you liked when you were a child.

What is your favorite TV show?

What is a good part-time job for a high school student? a university student?

What is a store that you like? What does it sell? What other buildings are near it?

Talk about a favorite relative. Why do you like him or her?

What activities do you usually do first in the morning and last at night?

Close your eyes. Describe your classroom. Say as much as you can in one minute.

What is a food you like but don't eat often? Why?

What numbers are lucky or unlucky in your culture?

Who is your favorite singer? What is your favorite song?

Recommend a job for each member of your group.

What movies do you know that came from books? Have you both seen and read them?

How do people in your culture celebrate birthdays? Tell about several customs.

What are some popular wedding gifts in your culture? What gifts are not appropriate?

What do you like to do on Sundays?

What is your favorite color? What clothes do you own in that color?

What can you say when you want someone to repeat something?

Say three things about a member of your family.

How many pieces of furniture can you name in English in one minute?

What buildings are near the school where you have your English class?

Imagine you're inventing a machine. What can it do?

How many spaces?					
2	1	3	4	3	5
5	3	4	2	3	1
3	1	2	5	4	3
1	2	4	3	5	2
3	5	2	1	4	3
2	1	3	4	3	5

Imagine you're introducing yourself to your friend's father. Tell three interesting things about yourself.

Who is your favorite movie star?

What machine do you use the most? How often do you use it?

Tell about a wonderful gift you received. Who gave it to you? What was it like?

Describe a holiday you don't like very much.

Is there a popular movie or TV show that you don't like? Why don't you like it?

What is your favorite number? Why?

How many pieces of furniture are in your room? Where are they?

What brands of clothing do you like? What brands don't you like? Why?

Imagine you're introducing yourself to an 8-year-old child. Tell three interesting things about yourself.

Listening tips

Here are some listening tips to help you become an active listener.

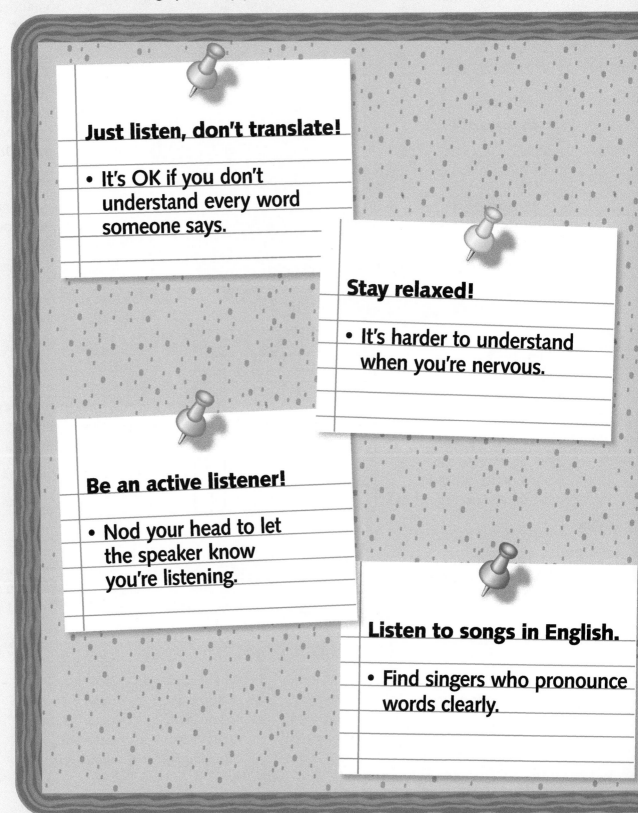

Just listen, don't translate!

- It's OK if you don't understand every word someone says.

Stay relaxed!

- It's harder to understand when you're nervous.

Be an active listener!

- Nod your head to let the speaker know you're listening.

Listen to songs in English.

- Find singers who pronounce words clearly.

Watch movies in English.

- Watch movies you've already seen in your native language.

Use the phone to practice English.

- Ask friends who are studying English to call you on the phone.

Call places with answering machines in English.

- Call several times for listening practice.

Listen to radio or news programs in English.

- Write down a few new words you don't understand. Then look them up.

Unit 1

A 1. 🎧 Listen to the conversation.

2. 🎧 Listen again. Circle the correct answers.

1. Luis and Emi are
   a. friends.
   b. meeting for the first time.

2. Luis is
   a. a student.
   b. a teacher.

3. Emi is studying
   a. English.
   b. music.

4. Emi likes
   a. all kinds of music.
   b. only classical music.

5. Luis likes
   a. classical music.
   b. pop music.

B 🎧 Listen. Check (✓) yes or no. Then write your answers.

	yes	no	
1.	☐	☐	_____
2.	☐	☐	_____
3.	☐	☐	_____
4.	☐	☐	_____
5.	☐	☐	_____

Unit 2

A **1.** 🎧 **Listen to the conversation.**

2. 🎧 **Listen again. Circle the correct answers.**

1. Andy has
   a. a brother and two sisters.
   b. a sister and a brother.

2. His sister Lisa is
   a. older.
   b. younger.

3. His brother Sam is
   a. older.
   b. younger.

4. Sam is
   a. a student.
   b. a doctor.

5. The woman has
   a. a sister.
   b. no brothers or sisters.

B 🎧 **Listen. Write your answers. You need to know these shapes:**
circle = ●   diamond = ◆   square = ■   star = ★

Unit 3

A **1.** 🎧 Listen to the conversation.

2. 🎧 Listen again. Circle the correct answers.

1. The man's date of birth is
   a. 11/12/87.
   b. 11/20/87.

2. His current number is
   a. 802-555-2646.
   b. 802-555-2466.

3. The man is buying
   a. a home phone.
   b. a cell phone.

4. His new number is
   a. 415-555-8953.
   b. 415-555-9835.

5. This is the man's
   a. first cell phone.
   b. second cell phone.

B 🎧 Listen. Write your answers.

Unit 4

A **1.** 🎧 Listen to the conversation.

2. 🎧 Listen again. Circle the correct answers.

1. The man is going to
   a. work.
   b. the store.
   c. a restaurant.

2. The man
   a. liked the chicken.
   b. didn't like the chicken.
   c. doesn't want to eat chicken again.

3. The woman will cook chicken again
   a. for lunch.
   b. tomorrow.
   c. next week.

4. Tonight, they will eat
   a. sandwiches and salad.
   b. pizza and salad.
   c. pasta and salad.

5. For dessert, they'll have
   a. lemon cake.
   b. melon.
   c. ice cream.

B 🎧 Listen. A server is taking your order. What is she asking about? Write the food. Then check (✓) your order.

1. _drink_

   ☐ tea   ☐ soda   ☐ water

2. _____

   ☐ fresh vegetable   ☐ pasta   ☐ chicken

3. _____

   ☐ mushroom   ☐ onion   ☐ tomato

4. _____

   ☐ chicken   ☐ tomatoes   ☐ mushrooms

5. _____

   ☐ vanilla   ☐ lemon   ☐ strawberry

Unit 5

A 1. 🎧 Listen to the information.

2. 🎧 Listen again. Circle the correct answers.

1. The man's friend Jack lives
   a. in another city.
   b. in the same city.
   c. in the same apartment building.

2. On Thursdays, the man
   a. works.
   b. stays home.
   c. goes out.

3. The man
   a. likes dancing.
   b. doesn't like dancing.
   c. has never tried dancing.

4. On Saturday, they
   a. played basketball.
   b. went to a basketball game.
   c. watched basketball on TV.

5. On Sunday, they had lunch
   a. at home.
   b. in a Chinese restaurant.
   c. with friends.

B 🎧 Listen. Check (✓) *yes* or *no*. Then write your answers.

	yes	no	
1.	☐	☐	_____
2.	☐	☐	_____
3.	☐	☐	_____
4.	☐	☐	_____
5.	☐	☐	_____

Unit 6

A **1.** 🎧 **Listen to the conversation.**

2. 🎧 **Listen again. Circle the correct answers.**

1. The people are talking about things
   a. they need to buy.
   b. they see in a store.
   c. they will bring on vacation.

2. The woman thinks the man has
   a. enough things.
   b. too many things.
   c. too few things.

3. They are going to
   a. the mountains.
   b. the beach.
   c. the city.

4. The man is going to take
   a. two jackets.
   b. one sweater.
   c. two sweaters.

5. The man thinks the woman has
   a. enough things.
   b. too many things.
   c. too few things.

B 🎧 **Listen. Check (✓) yes or no. Then write your answers.**

	yes	no	
1.	☐	☐	_____
2.	☐	☐	_____
3.	☐	☐	_____
4.	☐	☐	_____
5.	☐	☐	_____

Unit 7

A **1.** 🎧 **Listen to the conversation.**

2. 🎧 **Listen again. Circle the correct answers.**

1. The people are talking about
   a. the woman's apartment.
   b. the man's apartment.
   c. a friend's apartment.

2. The woman's new couch is
   a. green.
   b. blue.
   c. blue and green.

3. The woman is going to give the man
   a. a new chair.
   b. her old chair.
   c. her old couch.

4. The woman also bought
   a. a coffee table.
   b. a table and chairs.
   c. a desk.

5. The woman's old rug
   a. was too small.
   b. was too big.
   c. didn't match the couch.

B 🎧 **Listen. You are going to draw things in a room. Follow the instructions.**

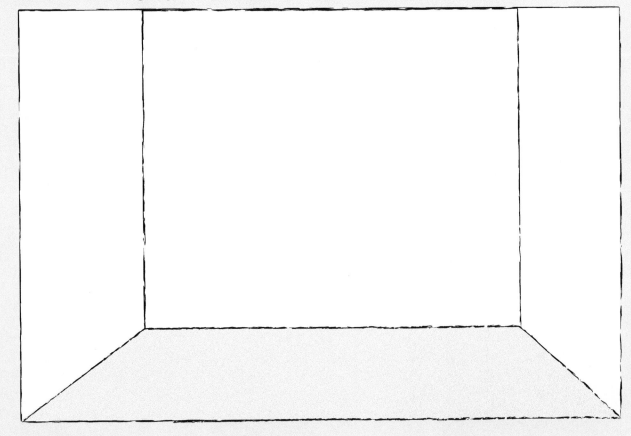

Unit 8

A **1.** 🎧 **Listen to the conversation.**

2. 🎧 **Listen again. Circle the correct answers.**

1. The people are talking about planning
   a. a trip.
   b. a party.
   c. a dinner.

2. The man finishes work at
   a. 5:00.
   b. 5:30.
   c. 6:00.

3. On Wednesday, the man is going to have
   a. a meeting.
   b. a party.
   c. dinner with a friend.

4. The woman can meet next
   a. Tuesday morning.
   b. Thursday morning.
   c. Tuesday afternoon.

5. The people are going to meet
   a. tomorrow morning.
   b. in two weeks.
   c. right now.

B 🎧 **Listen. Check (✓) yes or no. Then write your answers.**

	yes	no	
1.	☐	☐	_____
2.	☐	☐	_____
3.	☐	☐	_____
4.	☐	☐	_____
5.	☐	☐	_____

Unit 9

A 1. 🎧 **Listen to the conversation.**

2. 🎧 **Listen again. Circle the correct answers.**

1. The people are going to
   a. a video store.
   b. a restaurant.
   c. a movie theater.

2. The woman doesn't like movies with
   a. silly situations.
   b. car chases.
   c. robots.

3. The man likes
   a. musicals.
   b. romances.
   c. horror movies.

4. They both like
   a. comedies.
   b. science fiction.
   c. action movies.

5. They are going to the movie at
   a. 7:00.
   b. 7:30.
   c. 9:30.

B 🎧 **Listen. Check (✓) *yes* or *no*. Then write your answers.**

	yes	no	
1.	☐	☐	_____
2.	☐	☐	_____
3.	☐	☐	_____
4.	☐	☐	_____
5.	☐	☐	_____

Unit 10

A 1. 🎧 **Listen to the conversation.**

2. 🎧 **Listen again. Circle the correct answers.**

1. The man can't find time to
   a. take a class.
   b. work at a part-time job.
   c. study for class.

2. The man gets up at
   a. 7:00.
   b. 8:00.
   c. 9:00.

3. He gets up, and then he
   a. has a cup of coffee.
   b. uses his computer.
   c. eats breakfast.

4. On TV, the man watches
   a. the news.
   b. a sports show.
   c. movies.

5. The woman thinks the man shouldn't
   a. work so hard.
   b. take so many classes.
   c. take so many breaks.

B 🎧 **Listen. Check (✓) *yes* or *no*. Then write your answers.**

	yes	no	
1.	☐	☐	_____
2.	☐	☐	_____
3.	☐	☐	_____
4.	☐	☐	_____
5.	☐	☐	_____

Unit 11

A **1.** Listen to the conversation.

2. Listen again. Circle the correct answers.

1. The woman is telling the man the location of
   a. a restaurant.
   b. a store.
   c. a bank.

2. The place the woman is talking about is
   a. in her hometown.
   b. in the city.
   c. near the man's house.

3. The bank is across from
   a. the restaurant.
   b. the art museum.
   c. the coffee shop.

4. The coffee shop is
   a. to the left of the restaurant.
   b. to the right of the restaurant.
   c. across from the restaurant.

5. The restaurant is between a clothing store and
   a. a Chinese restaurant.
   b. a bank.
   c. a bookstore.

B Listen. Complete the sentences with your answers.

1. I _____ .

2. I see _____ .

3. I _____ .

4. I _____ .

5. I see _____ .

Unit 12

A **1.** 🎧 **Listen to the conversation.**

2. 🎧 **Listen again. Circle the correct answers.**

1. The people are talking about
   a. the man's friends.
   b. the woman's friends.
   c. both of their friends.

2. The man is going to
   a. go to the wedding.
   b. bring a gift.
   c. send a gift.

3. The man thinks a kitchen gift is
   a. a perfect gift.
   b. an unlucky gift.
   c. not a good gift.

4. The man thinks a picture is
   a. too hard to choose.
   b. something they wouldn't like.
   c. something they don't need.

5. The woman thinks the man should give
   a. a gift certificate.
   b. cash.
   c. furniture.

B 🎧 **Listen. Follow the instructions.**

1. ☐ make something   ☐ buy something

2. ☐ something from my country   ☐ something from another country

3. ☐ flowers   ☐ chocolate   ☐ something else: _____

4. ☐ some money   ☐ some CDs   ☐ something else: _____

5. _____

Unit 13

A **1.** 🎧 **Listen to the conversation.**

2. 🎧 **Listen again. Circle the correct answers.**

1. The people are talking about
   a. summer jobs.
   b. a trip they took.
   c. jobs after graduation.

2. The man worked last year as
   a. a porter.
   b. a tour guide.
   c. a server.

3. The woman
   a. enjoyed being a server.
   b. did not enjoy being a server.
   c. is a server now.

4. The man thinks being a porter would be
   a. OK.
   b. bad.
   c. boring.

5. The man will probably look for a job as
   a. a porter.
   b. a clerk.
   c. a server.

B 🎧 **Listen. Answer the job interview questions. Check (✓) yes or no.**

	yes	no
1.	☐	☐
2.	☐	☐
3.	☐	☐
4.	☐	☐
5.	☐	☐

Unit 14

A **1.** 🎧 **Listen to the conversation.**

2. 🎧 **Listen again. Circle the correct answers.**

1. The people are talking about their
   a. next vacation.
   b. last vacation.
   c. favorite vacation.

2. The man thinks visiting relatives is
   a. relaxing.
   b. a bad vacation.
   c. a good vacation.

3. The woman is going to
   a. eat special food.
   b. see a parade.
   c. get presents.

4. The man is going to
   a. visit relatives.
   b. visit New York.
   c. stay home and work.

5. The people are
   a. office workers.
   b. students.
   c. tour guides.

B 🎧 **Listen. Follow the instructions.**

1. _____

	yes	no	
2.	☐	☐	_____
3.	☐	☐	_____
4.	☐	☐	_____
5.	☐	☐	_____

Unit 15

A **1.** 🎧 **Listen to the conversation.**

2. 🎧 **Listen again. Circle the correct answers.**

1. The man has to
   a. fix his computer.
   b. do some homework.
   c. take a test.

2. The woman thinks the assignment is
   a. too difficult.
   b. not difficult.
   c. not very interesting.

3. The woman thinks everybody will write about
   a. computers.
   b. clocks.
   c. calendars.

4. The man doesn't know much about
   a. clocks or calendars.
   b. inventions.
   c. computers.

5. The woman's favorite invention is
   a. the clock.
   b. the calendar.
   c. chocolate.

B 🎧 **Listen. Check (✓) your guesses to the Inventions Quiz. Then listen to the correct answers. Did you guess correctly?**

1. ☐ 1776   ☐ 1848   ☐ 1904

2. ☐ the U.S.   ☐ France   ☐ England

3. ☐ 1623   ☐ 1755   ☐ 1815

4. ☐ eyeglasses   ☐ bicycles   ☐ telephones

5. ☐ Japan   ☐ Germany   ☐ the U.S.

Unit 16

A 1. 🎧 **Listen to the conversation.**

2. 🎧 **Listen again. Circle the correct answers.**

1. The people are talking about
   a. renting a movie.
   b. going to a movie.
   c. making a movie.

2. The woman's movie will probably have
   a. magic.
   b. car chases.
   c. robots.

3. The man thinks Adam will be
   a. a bad prince.
   b. a good prince.
   c. a good farmer.

4. The man thinks Jason will be
   a. a good prince.
   b. a good farmer.
   c. a bad farmer.

5. The woman wants the man to
   a. film the movie.
   b. be a prince in the movie.
   c. be a farmer in the movie.

B 🎧 **Listen to the story. Imagine the scene. Then listen again. Write the missing words on the lines.**

A (long) road went __through__ a (_____) _____ .

A (_____) _____ was _____ down

the _____ . Suddenly she _____ a (_____) _____ .

He was _____ a (_____) _____ ,

(_____) _____ , and a (_____) _____ .

He _____ and _____ , (" _____ .")

C 🎧 **Listen again. When you hear the bell, write any word in the circle that makes sense. You can choose any word you want.**

Self-study answer key

For multiple-choice items in Exercise A and set items in Exercise B.

Unit 1

Exercise A

1. b
2. a
3. b
4. a
5. b

Unit 2

Exercise A

1. b
2. a
3. a
4. a
5. b

Unit 3

Exercise A

1. b
2. a
3. b
4. b
5. a

Unit 4

Exercise A

1. b
2. a
3. c
4. c
5. b

Exercise B

1. drink
2. salad
3. soup
4. pizza (topping)
5. dessert (cake)

Unit 5

Exercise A

1. a
2. b
3. b
4. a
5. c

Unit 6

Exercise A

1. c
2. c
3. a
4. b
5. b

Unit 7

Exercise A

1. a
2. b
3. c
4. a
5. c

Exercise B

Unit 8

Exercise A

1. b   4. a
2. a   5. c
3. c

Unit 9
Exercise A
1. c
2. b
3. c
4. a
5. b

Unit 10
Exercise A
1. c
2. b
3. a
4. b
5. c

Unit 11
Exercise A
1. a
2. b
3. b
4. c
5. c

Unit 12
Exercise A
1. a
2. c
3. c
4. a
5. b

Unit 13
Exercise A
1. a
2. c
3. b
4. a
5. b

Unit 14
Exercise A
1. a
2. c
3. a
4. b
5. a

Unit 15
Exercise A
1. b
2. b
3. a
4. a
5. c
Exercise B
1. 1904
2. France
3. 1755
4. eyeglasses
5. the U.S.

Unit 16
Exercise A
1. c
2. a
3. b
4. c
5. c
Exercise B
A ( ) road went **through** a ( ) **forest**. A
( ) **woman** was **walking** down the **road**.
Suddenly she **saw** a ( ) **man**. He was
wearing a ( ) **shirt**, ( ) **pants**, and a ( )
hat. He **smiled** and **said**, ("   .")

Self-study track listing

The audio CD contains the Self-study audio exercises from Student's Book 1.

Track	Unit	Page
Track 1	Unit 1	Page 84
Track 2	Unit 2	Page 85
Track 3	Unit 3	Page 86
Track 4	Unit 4	Page 87
Track 5	Unit 5	Page 88
Track 6	Unit 6	Page 89
Track 7	Unit 7	Page 90
Track 8	Unit 8	Page 91
Track 9	Unit 9	Page 92
Track 10	Unit 10	Page 93
Track 11	Unit 11	Page 94
Track 12	Unit 12	Page 95
Track 13	Unit 13	Page 96
Track 14	Unit 14	Page 97
Track 15	Unit 15	Page 98
Track 16	Unit 16	Page 99